Exploring TECHNOLOGY

5

Glass and Glassmaking–Leather

Marshall Cavendish
New York • London • Toronto • Sydney

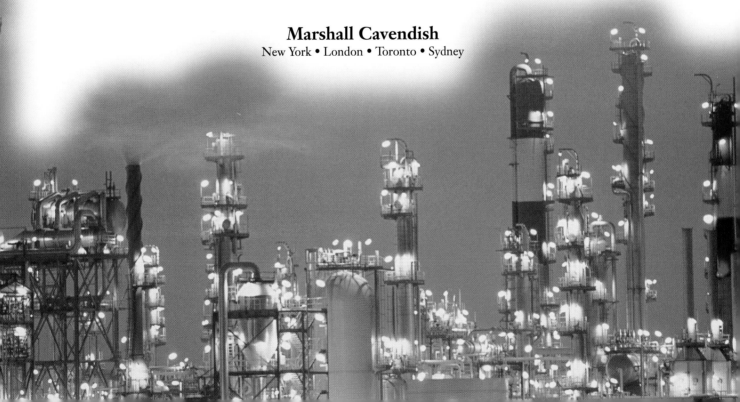

Marshall Cavendish
99 White Plains Road
Tarrytown, New York 10591

www.marshallcavendish.com

© 2004 Marshall Cavendish Corporation

Created by **The Brown Reference Group plc**

Library of Congress Cataloging-in-Publication Data

Exploring technology.
    p. cm.
    Includes bibliographical references and index.
  Contents: v. 1. ABR-BIC -- v. 2. BIO-COG -- v. 3. COL-END -- v. 4.
ENE-GEO -- v. 5. GLA-LEA -- v. 6. LIG-MOV -- v. 7. MUL-POT -- v. 8.
POW-SHI -- v. 9. SHI-TEL -- v. 10. TEL-WOO -- v. 11. Index.
  ISBN 0-7614-7406-4 (set)
  1. Technology--Encyclopedias.
  T9 .E97 2003
  603--dc21

            2002071510

   ISBN 0-7614-7406-4 (set)
   ISBN 0-7614-7411-0 (vol 5)

Printed in China

08 07 06 05 04 03   5 4 3 2 1

PHOTOGRAPHIC CREDITS

Trevor Baylis: *375;* **Bethlehem Steel:** *378, 381, 383;* **Corbis:** Bettmann *366, 369,* Lloyd Cluff *358,*
Dean Conger *355,* Frank Lane Pictures *365,* Owen Franken *335,* Mark E. Gibson *368,* Ian Harward *359,*
Kelly-Mooney Photography *350,* Danny Lehman *398,* Roger Ressmeyer *346, 347, 370, 387, 388, 395,*
Leif Skoogfors *329,* Liba Taylor *364,* Roger Wood *340;* **Sylvia Cordaiy Photo Library:** Cees Van
Leeuwen *349;* **DaimlerChrysler Corp:** *376;* **Draper:** *330;* **Easy Everything:** *372;* **Ecoscene:** Andrew
Brown *339,* Martin Jones *361;* **Paul Falworth:** *325;* **Google:** *374;* **Image Bank:** *367;* **NASA:** *377,*
Kennedy Space Center *393, 394, 397;* **Newscast:** Boots Company Plc *390/1,* Vasser Thorncroft (UK)
Ltd *389;* **NRCS/USDA:** Lynn Betts *384,* Tim McCabe *332, 385,* Bob Nichols *351;* **Pacific Northwest
National Laboratory:** *334;* **Sharp Electronics Corp:** *353;* **Siemens AG:** *373;* **Transport Action:**
Ford Transit *356;* **Travel Ink:** Leslie Garland *352;* **TRH Pictures:** *344,* Edgeley Sail-Planes *327;*
U.S. Army: *342*

Front cover Leslie Garland Picture Library: Andrew Lambert
Title page Digital Vision
Contents page Digital Vision

MARSHALL CAVENDISH

Project editor: Peter Mavrikis
Production manager: Alan Tsai
Editorial director: Paul Bernabeo

THE BROWN REFERENCE GROUP PLC

Project editor: Clive Carpenter
Deputy editor: Jim Martin
Design: Richard Berry, Alison Gardner
Picture research: Helen Simm, Susannah Jayes, Rebecca Cox
Illustrations: Darren Awuah, Dax Fullbrook, Mark Walker
Index: Kay Ollerenshaw
Managing editor: Bridget Giles

Exploring TECHNOLOGY

5

GLA-LEA

Glass and Glassmaking	324	Horticulture	348	Internet	372
Glider	327	Household Appliances	352	Inventions	375
Global Positioning System	328	Hovercraft	354	Iron and Steel	378
		Hydraulics	356	Irrigation	384
Hand Tools	330	Hydroelectricity	358	Laser	388
Harvesting Machinery	332	Hydrofoil	360	Launch Site	392
Hazardous Waste	334	Ignition System	362	Launch Vehicle	395
Heart-lung Machine	335	Immunology	364	Leather	398
Heat Exchanger	337	Information Theory	367	GLOSSARY	399
Heating Systems	338	Insulation	368	INDEX	400
Helicopter	342	Integrated Circuit	369		
Holography	345	Intensive Care Unit	371		

Marshall Cavendish
New York • London • Toronto • Sydney

Glass and Glassmaking

A see-through material that allows light to pass through or be reflected

Although the glass in a windowpane or a vase is solid, when it is produced it is a hot, runny liquid, and although the glass cools down, it retains many fluidlike properties. For example, glass is see-through. The atoms (the smallest particles of matter) of most solid substances are bound together in structures called crystals. Light is absorbed by crystals. Due to its liquid properties, glass does not have a crystalline structure, so light can pass through.

The fluid nature of glass also makes it very strong. Glass can carry large weights, although it will break with a sudden impact. Many types of glass are made, and many everyday objects are made of glass. These include television and computer screens, drinking glasses, and window panes. Glass is also used in a variety of less familiar roles, in electronic components, insulation, and in fiber optic cables.

HIGHLIGHTS

◆ Silica, or sand, is the principal ingredient of glass. Other materials are added to produce glass with different properties.

◆ Glassblowing was the most important method for making glass until the 20th century.

◆ Blowing is now done by machines. Furnaces have revolutionized the production of sheet glass.

Traditional glassmaking

Glass is made from the mineral silica (SIH-lih-kuh). The most common source of silica for glassmaking is sand. Sand is very hard to melt and forms crystals as it cools, so glassmakers add limestone and soda to keep the silica liquid for a longer period during cooling. This mixture of minerals melts at about 1560°F (850°C).

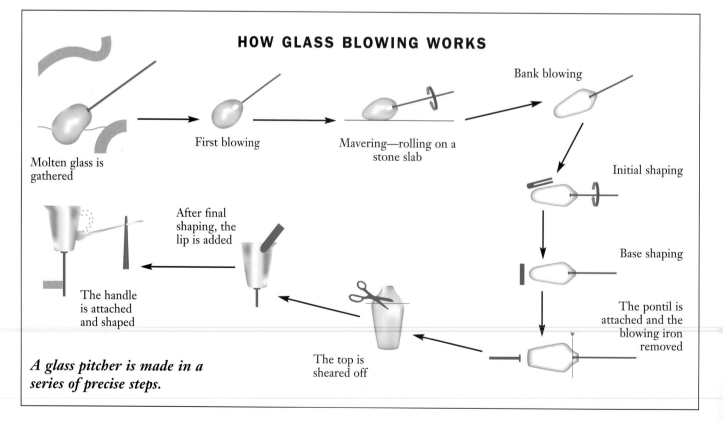

HOW GLASS BLOWING WORKS

Molten glass is gathered

First blowing

Mavering—rolling on a stone slab

Bank blowing

Initial shaping

Base shaping

The pontil is attached and the blowing iron removed

The top is sheared off

The handle is attached and shaped

After final shaping, the lip is added

A glass pitcher is made in a series of precise steps.

The ancient Egyptians were the first people to make glass, around 6,000 years ago. They, and glassmakers from many later civilizations, carved blocks or beads of glass straight from the molten mineral mixture. However, contact between the carving tool and the hot glass spoiled the transparency of the final product.

Babylonian glassmakers invented the blowing iron in about 200 B.C.E. This revolutionized glassmaking. The blowing iron is still sometimes used to make glass vessels. A glassworker blows into the tube at one end of the iron. The blast of breath into the blowing iron shapes the molten glass held at the other end of the tube. Each breath makes the molten glass expand further to form a hollow vessel.

Blowing irons, however, can only be used to make round objects. A method, called the crown glass method, for making clear glass sheets was introduced into Europe from Syria in the 14th century. Glass panes were made from a large glass sphere created by a glassblower. The sphere was returned to the furnace to become soft again. It was then removed and spun at high speed. This flattened the glass out into flat sheets.

At the beginning of the Industrial Revolution in the 18th century, glassmaking became more automated. The invention of iron molds made it possible to create many copies of glass objects such as bottles and vases. Sheet glass was made by mechanically flattening blown molten glass.

The modern glass industry

Production of sheet glass underwent great changes in the 20th century. The quality of glass improved dramatically with the introduction of huge furnace tanks. Inside these tanks, which may measure up to 150 feet (45 m) long, the materials needed to make glass can be mixed thoroughly. The ingredients, called frit, are mixed with broken glass that helps the frit melt. Frit is mixed mechanically in the furnace, where temperatures reach 2900°F (1600°C).

Making sheet glass

There are several ways to make sheet glass. In the vertical draw process, a metal bar is laid between the walls of the furnace. The glass fuses to the bar, which is pulled upward, dragging a sheet of molten glass behind. The temperature of the sheet is then reduced slowly.

Thicker plate glass is made by casting molten glass onto metal tables. Contact with this solid surface during cooling reduces the transparency of the plate glass, so another method is often used. Molten glass is poured over molten tin in a tank. It spreads evenly across the tin's surface into flat sheets. Known as the float-glass process, this produces glass that has the transparency of vertically drawn glass with the thickness of plate glass.

Types of glass

Different types of glass are made by varying the ingredients. The addition of lead makes

Modern glass design often emphasizes the fluidlike properties of this solid.

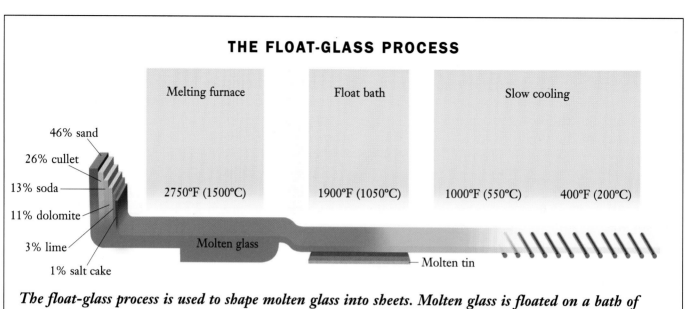

THE FLOAT-GLASS PROCESS

Melting furnace
2750°F (1500°C)

Float bath
1900°F (1050°C)

Slow cooling
1000°F (550°C)   400°F (200°C)

46% sand
26% cullet
13% soda
11% dolomite
3% lime
1% salt cake

Molten glass

Molten tin

The float-glass process is used to shape molten glass into sheets. Molten glass is floated on a bath of molten tin to form the sheet, cooling and hardening as it moves along the bath.

the glass highly transparent and soft to cut. This glass, called lead crystal, is used to make beautiful cut-glass products. Small flat areas, called facets, are cut into the lead crystal surface. The facets scatter light into the colors of the rainbow. Kitchenware is made from heat-resistant glass. Ordinary glass cracks when one side is heated more rapidly than the other. The heated side expands, causing stresses that can shatter the glass. In heat-resistant glass, silica is replaced by minerals that expand at a slower rate. This glass can be used safely in a hot oven.

There are many ways to stop sheets of glass from shattering. The simplest method is to sandwich a grid of reinforcing wires between two layers of glass. This reinforced glass loses some transparency. Laminated glass is used when it is important that the glass stays transparent. Instead of a wire sandwich, glass layers are bonded to a central plastic layer. Laminated glass is used in car windshields. The glass still shatters in an accident, but stays attached to the plastic filling.

Glass can be toughened by heat treatment. Sheet glass is heated until it becomes soft, then it is cooled gradually. This process, which is called annealing, eliminates areas of strain that might cause cracks. Chemical treatments can also strengthen glass, making it resistant to acids and other chemicals. This makes it useful for making laboratory glassware, which may come into

contact with many different chemicals. Recent technological advances allow glass to be drawn into extremely thin, extremely strong fibers. The discovery that these fibers reflect light internally, without any leaking out, has revolutionized telecommunications. These fiber optic cables are used in computers and in telecommunication lines under the ocean.

CHECK THESE OUT!
✔CASTING ✔CERAMICS ✔FIBER OPTICS ✔LIGHTING

PEOPLE

Carl Zeiss

German industrialist Carl Zeiss (1816–1888) was the first to develop a scientific approach to glassmaking. His name is still associated with high-quality optical instruments, such as microscopes and binoculars.

In 1846, Zeiss opened a factory in Jena, Germany. He hired physicist Ernst Abbe (1840–1905) and chemist Otto Schott (1851–1935) to help. Abbe worked out optical theories for microscopes and other devices, allowing them to be precision manufactured for the first time. Schott experimented with different types of glass. He patented more than 100 optical glasses, each with specific properties, and founded the Schott Glassworks.

Glider

Gliders were the ancestors of modern powered airplanes. However, unlike airplanes, gliders do not usually have engines. They remain airborne due to a force called lift, which is caused by the shape of the wings. Air moves more quickly over the upper surface than the lower surface, causing a pressure difference that pushes the glider upward and forward. A typical modern glider is made of lightweight materials such as aluminum alloys, fiberglass, and carbon fiber. It has long wings that provide lift.

Because lift alone is not able to overcome the combined forces of the weight of the aircraft and the drag (resistance of the air to movement), gliders gradually sink. To prolong a flight, glider pilots often use thermals—rising columns of warm air. Many animals that glide, such as vultures and storks, also use thermals.

Launch and flight

One way to launch a glider is to use a winch and cable. The winch sits at one end of an airstrip. The cable runs from the winch to a hook on the glider, which is at the other end of the strip. When the winch winds the cable in, it pulls the glider along with it. The glider picks up speed and climbs into the air. When the correct altitude (height) is reached, the hook automatically releases the cable, and the glider flies away.

Alternatively, some gliders are towed behind a truck, but to get more speed and height, most gliders now use powered tow airplanes. The tow airplane takes off from the ground, pulling the glider behind it. When the glider is high enough in the air, it disconnects from the towing line. A motorized glider can take off on its

own. It has a small engine and propeller to power it into the air. When it reaches the correct height, the pilot turns the engine off and the aircraft begins to glide.

Gliders change altitude and direction in the same way as powered aircraft, by altering the shape and angle of the wings and tail fins relative to the airflow. For example, struts on the wings called ailerons allow the glider to turn.

CHECK THESE OUT!
✔AERODYNAMICS ✔AIRCRAFT DESIGN
✔AIRPORT AND AIRFIELD
✔FLIGHT

> ## HIGHLIGHTS
>
> ◆ Gliders are unpowered aircraft with long wings that create a lot of lift.
>
> ◆ Most gliders use winches, tow trucks, or tow planes to get them airborne.
>
> ◆ Motorized gliders have small engines and take off under their own power.

An Edgeley EA9 glider soars over the English countryside.

Global Positioning System

A satellite system that provides accurate location information worldwide

In 1993, the U.S. Air Force launched the last of 24 Navstar satellites into orbit, 11,000 miles (17,600 km) above the surface of Earth. This satellite completed the installation of the Global Positioning System (GPS), a system that allows people with the correct technology to find out their exact location anywhere in the world. In civilian use, GPS is accurate to within around 300 feet (90 m). Military applications increase the accuracy to within 60 feet (18 m).

The development of GPS

Early mariners charted their courses using the stars. This had obvious drawbacks, since the stars could only be seen at night and then only in cloud-free skies. Later, magnetic compasses and sextants were used. Sextants used a series of mirrors to measure the positions of the Sun, Moon, and stars above the horizon. However,

Three satellites give a reasonable estimate of location, but four are required for increased accuracy.

HIGHLIGHTS 💡

◆ The GPS system incorporates 24 satellites that orbit the Earth.

◆ GPS is used for navigation at sea and on land.

◆ Using handheld GPS equipment, travelers can estimate their position on the globe to within 300 feet (90 m).

sextants were only useful for determining latitude (location north or south of the equator). Sailors had no way of knowing their longitude (location east or west around the globe). This problem was resolved by an English carpenter, John Harrison (1693–1776). Over many years, he developed an accurate timepiece called a chronometer (KRON-uh-muht-uhr). The chronometer lost very little time over weeks and months, and this, together with the sextant, allowed sailors to work out roughly where they were.

Ground-based radio navigation systems were developed and used during World War II (1939–1945). However, these systems were not accurate and did not work well over wide areas. Soon after the launch of the Soviet *Sputnik I* satellite in 1957, military scientists realized that the only way to provide an accurate navigation system for the entire globe was by using satellite technology. In 1978, the first U.S. Navstar satellite was sent into orbit.

How GPS works

Each Navstar satellite weighs around 1,900 pounds (860 kg) and measures about 17 feet (5.2 m) across. The satellites are powered by a series of solar panels. Each GPS satellite makes a complete circuit of Earth in 12 hours. Each satellite must stay in exactly the same orbit for the system to work, and the positions of the satellites are monitored constantly. Their altitude (height) prevents the atmosphere from affecting their flight path, and the influence of gravity from the Moon can easily be compensated for. GPS relies on the accuracy of atomic clocks. Based on the oscillations (wobbles) of a cesium atom, the atomic clocks used in the GPS program are extraordinarily accurate. It would take 20 million years for these clocks to lose or gain one second of time.

A soldier uses GPS equipment while on maneuvers.

LOOK CLOSER

Uses of GPS

GPS is important for mapmakers, and navigators at sea, as well as for lost explorers. The GPS system now provides travel information for motorists and helps ambulance crews to be allocated swiftly to an emergency. The system was also important during the construction of the Channel Tunnel, which links England and France. It helped the tunnelers keep on course to meet at the halfway point.

Each satellite continuously broadcasts a digital high-frequency radio signal that includes both its own position and the exact time in the form of a code. Each satellite has four atomic clocks onboard, and an average time reading is sent, further increasing the incredible accuracy. As the orbits of the satellites are monitored, their precise altitude, speed, and position are recorded, and the information is sent back to the satellites. This data is incorporated into the code.

Lost in a forest

The satellites are arrayed in space so that, at any one time, every point on the planet is within radio contact of four of them. An explorer in the rain forest may have a handheld GPS receiver. Radio waves travel at the speed of light (187,700 miles/299,800 km per second). Despite this great speed, there is a measurable "lag" between the time a message is sent by the satellite and the time it is received. The explorer's receiver calculates the time difference and figures out how far away the GPS satellite is. The distance is equal to the time difference in seconds multiplied by the speed of light.

Information from four satellites allows the receiver to pinpoint the explorer's exact latitude and longitude. For the system to work properly, the receiver has to know exactly where the satellites are, and the satellites must keep reliable and extremely accurate time.

CHECK THESE OUT!
✔MARITIME COMMUNICATION ✔NAVIGATION

Hand Tools

Portable instruments used to perform manual tasks

Humans are one of the few animals to use tools. Tools helped early people hunt, grow crops, and build homes. The first tools were made from stones, such as flint, and wood. When handles were added to tools, work could be done with more force and accuracy, and when metal tools replaced stone, a variety of new tools could be made.

The first metal tools were made of copper. Bronze, which is stronger than copper, began to replace that metal around 3000 B.C.E. Iron replaced bronze 2,000 years later and became the main material for tool making. The amount of carbon in iron changes the properties of the metal. Steel, which has a high carbon content, is one of the most useful types of iron. Early steel was expensive and could not be made cheaply until the 19th century. Before the Industrial Revolution in the 18th century, tools were custom-made by blacksmiths. Individual blacksmiths had their own styles. Factory-made tools reduced the variations in basic hand tools.

Uses of hand tools

Some of the earliest tools were used in food preparation, to crack nuts, butcher animals, and for other tasks. Stones were chipped away to create cutting edges to make knives.

Strokes with a plane, like this one, cut thin shavings from a wood surface.

Hunting tools have a long history. Sharp wooden spears more than 400,000 years old have been found. The bow and arrow and the atlatl, a stick with a socket to help hunters launch spears, are just as ancient.

The first farming tool was a digging stick to unearth roots and tubers. Modern hunter-gatherers use similar tools. When crop farming developed, tools such as the plow, hoe, and scythe appeared. The scythe has a long curved blade to cut crops in the harvest.

HIGHLIGHTS

- ◆ The first hand tools were made from stone.

- ◆ Before the 18th century, hand tools were custom-made made by blacksmiths.

- ◆ Many modern tools are powered by electricity.

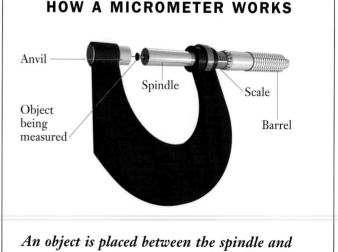

HOW A MICROMETER WORKS

Anvil

Spindle

Scale

Object being measured

Barrel

An object is placed between the spindle and anvil, and the barrel is wound until the object is held tightly. The width is read on the scale.

Early civilizations built large structures from stone that had been shaped with simple tools such as chisels, wedges, and fire. Large blocks were moved using levers, wedges, and rollers. The pyramids in Egypt were built in this way.

Working wood and metal

Wood was first worked with stone tools and fire. Knives were used for small cuts. Stone axes and wedges split wood. The first metal tools were the axe and the adze. The adze, which has a cutting blade at right angles to the handle, was used to chop down trees and shape surfaces. Chisels cut holes in wood and refine shapes. They have sharpened edges on metal blades. Most modern chisels are made from steel.

Early drills were pointed sticks held in one hand and rotated. A string wrapped around the stick was attached to a bow. Moving the bow backward and forward turned the drill. A piece of stone attached to the end of the stick helped drill into harder materials.

The first saws were strips of metal held under tension. Serrated (jagged) edges made a more effective cutting blade. In time, many different hand tools for woodworking were developed, including hammers, planes (used to smooth a wood surface), and bradawls, which make holes for nails. For thousands of years, the main tools for shaping metal were the forge, anvil, and hammer used by blacksmiths. When large machines started to be used, new tools such as wrenches, pliers, and screwdrivers were created. Saws and chisels for cutting metal were developed from woodworking tools. Files were made in large numbers only after the development of cheap steel in the 19th century.

Tools with cutting edges must be sharpened. Flint tools were sharpened by flaking off pieces of the stone, using another stone. Metal tools are sharpened using an abrasive stone such as novaculite (no-VAHK-yuh-lyt). In ancient times, sand was used to smooth and polish wood. Modern sandpaper developed from this practice.

Measuring tools

To design buildings and furniture, it is important to measure angles and lengths. Levels, plumb lines, and measuring string were used by the

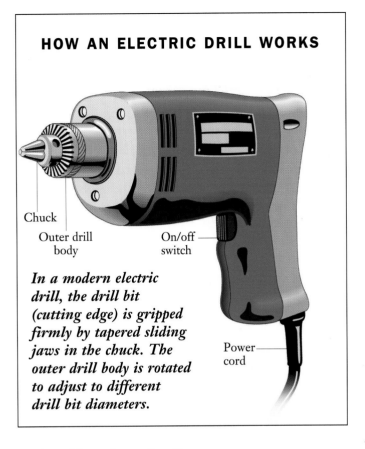

HOW AN ELECTRIC DRILL WORKS

Chuck

Outer drill body

On/off switch

Power cord

In a modern electric drill, the drill bit (cutting edge) is gripped firmly by tapered sliding jaws in the chuck. The outer drill body is rotated to adjust to different drill bit diameters.

ancient Egyptians. Smaller measurements were made using calipers and compasses. As machinery developed, it became necessary to make accurate, repeatable measurements. The micrometer measures very small distances. A fine screw and nut on a micrometer are turned to measure less than one-thousandth of an inch.

CHECK THESE OUT!
✔CROP FARMING ✔FASTENING AND JOINING ✔MEASUREMENT ✔METALS ✔WOOD AND WOOD CARVING

LOOK CLOSER

Power tools

The development of small electric motors gave a power source to hand tools. Metal drills, held in a chuck attached to an electric motor, drill through wood or metal faster than hand-powered tools. Electric power tools are small versions of larger stationary power tools. Circular saws, for example, are small versions of timber-factory tools originally powered by steam.

Harvesting Machinery

Machinery used to gather crops, including cereals

Thousands of years ago, early humans developed hand tools to harvest cereals such as wheat, barley, and rice. The first tools were flint blades. The Egyptians used sickles with curved metal blades. Later, the Romans added long handles to blades to make a scythe, which made cutting quicker and meant less stooping. Blades were made larger, producing a wider cut.

When harvesting cereals, farmers separated the grain from the straw (stalks) by beating the cut crop with a tool called a flail. This consisted of a free-swinging stick attached to a wooden handle. Hand-held sickles and flails are still used to harvest crops in many parts of the world.

The first harvesting machines

In the early 19th century, engineers in North America and Europe invented machines to reduce the hard work of harvesting. Small machines were developed to separate the grain from the straw, a process known as threshing. However, the chaff (husks) and other waste still had to be separated by tossing the crop into the air and allowing the wind to blow the waste away. This process is called winnowing. The 1830s saw the development of several harvesting machines that combined the processes of cutting and gathering. The most famous was the McCormick reaper, designed by U.S. inventor Cyrus Hall McCormick (1809–1884). This horse-drawn reaper was operated by a two-person crew. It could cut and bundle as much grain as 12 to 16 people using hand tools.

By the late 19th century, harvesting machines that could thresh and winnow grain crops were developed. They were pulled from field to field by horses or large, steam-powered tractors. They were heavy, expensive, and not adaptable.

Combine harvesters

In many countries, cereal crops are harvested by machines called combine harvesters or combines. These machines earned their

Combines, such as this one in Iowa, clean the harvested grain, then pass it through an augur into a waiting truck or wagon.

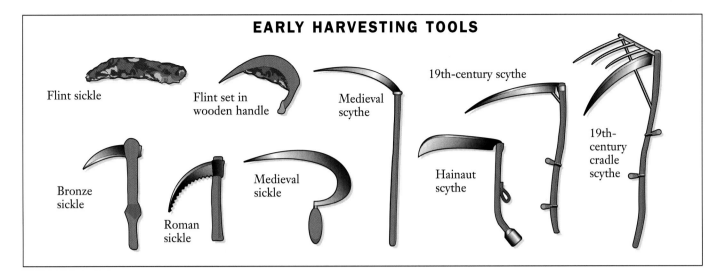

EARLY HARVESTING TOOLS

Flint sickle

Flint set in wooden handle

Medieval scythe

19th-century scythe

Bronze sickle

Roman sickle

Medieval sickle

Hainaut scythe

19th-century cradle scythe

name because they combine all five basic harvesting operations: cutting, threshing, sieving, cleaning, and gathering the crop. Cereals, grasses, beans, peas, and seed crops can all be harvested by combines.

Some combines are pulled and powered by tractors, but most are self-powered. Cabs contain many controls that allow farmers to adjust the equipment to cope with different crops and field conditions. Most modern cabs are equipped with sensors to gather information about crop yield and quality.

How combines work

Combines contain different devices to process crops. A device called the header gathers, cuts, and feeds the crop into the threshing unit as it moves through the field. The threshing unit is usually a rotating cylinder with metal rasp bars, surrounded by a metal cover called a concave. The cylinder rotates at speeds of up to 1,500 revolutions each minute to separate the grain from the straw.

The grain then passes through another threshing device called a beater. This shakes it to remove more waste. Grain then passes through a separator that contains a series of moving metal racks, which have small openings to let grain fall through. The small quantity of chaff and weeds still mixed with the grain are removed in the cleaning unit. This consists of a fan that blows air through two sieving devices. The light chaff is blown away, while the heavier, cleaned grain passes through and is fed into the grain tank.

Grasses and forage crops

Grasses and crops such as clover and alfalfa are grown to feed farm livestock. They are usually made into hay or silage by machinery that cuts, processes, packages, and moves the crop. Silage is fodder made from moist, green crops, such as grass and clover, which are fermented by bacteria in airtight conditions. Rotary mowers, flail mowers, and rotary choppers are used to cut and process these crops. Sometimes the crop is cured, or dried, to make it easier to store. Mechanical balers scoop up the crop and compress it before binding it with twine. Grasses and forage crops are often stored in buildings called silos.

CHECK THESE OUT!
✔CROP FARMING ✔FARM STORAGE ✔TRACTOR

LOOK CLOSER

Harvesting fruit and vegetables

Crops such as carrots, potatoes, and radishes can be harvested and delivered to the supermarket without ever being touched by human hands. Many fruits that are grown in big, commercial orchards are also harvested by machines. However, small, independent farmers cannot afford to buy expensive equipment. Fragile citrus fruit are still labor-intensive to harvest. Fruits like these, as well as many vegetables, remain the only crops in North America that are regularly harvested by hand.

Hazardous Waste

Garbage and by-products that can harm people or the environment

Different waste presents different risks. Toxic wastes are chemical poisons. Some are acute (fast acting). Others have chronic (long-term) effects, causing illnesses such as cancer. Some waste has a cumulative (growing) toxic effect on the environment. It breaks down very slowly, and the concentration of poison increases over a number of years. Waste products that react violently with other elements may explode or cause fires. Some hazardous waste is corrosive, attacking other materials.

Clinical or biomedical waste, such as syringes (suh-RINJ-uhs), bandages, or human tissue, is produced in hospitals and laboratories. This waste is hazardous because it carries bacteria and other disease-causing organisms. Radioactive waste can damage living tissue and cause cancers. Most radioactive waste comes from nuclear power stations or weapons testing.

Managing hazardous waste

Some hazardous waste has to be stored before it is disposed of. Solid waste must be protected from the wind so it is not dispersed. It must be stored on a watertight base so it cannot dissolve and soak into the soil. Liquid waste is stored in shallow ponds called lagoons. Liquids that evaporate easily are kept in tanks. The tanks must be made from suitable materials, without leaks. Chemicals that dissolve other materials are called solvents. They are stored in steel vessels. Liquids that react with metals are stored in plastic drums. Waste gases are not stored but are treated as they are produced.

Hazardous waste disposal

Waste can be recycled (used again), destroyed, or stored. Toxic, reactive, and radioactive waste can all be recycled. It is purified and used for other processes. Chemicals are added to reactive waste to neutralize it and create new materials. Some waste is destroyed by incineration (burning). Incineration is controlled to ensure that poisonous gases are not released into the air.

Solid waste may be buried in pits called landfill sites. These are monitored to ensure that toxic waste does not seep into the soil or water supply. Some liquid waste is injected into layers of sandstone deep underground.

Radioactive waste is classed as low-, medium-, or high-level waste depending on the amount of radiation it emits (gives off). Low-level waste can be buried in landfill. High-level waste, including spent (used) fuel rods from nuclear power stations, can emit radiation for centuries. This waste is cast into glass blocks, which are placed in tunnels that run at least 300 feet (100 m) beneath the ground. The tunnels are then filled and sealed.

A radioactive waste tank in Hanford, Washington.

CHECK THESE OUT!
✔ CANCER TREATMENTS
✔ CHEMICAL INDUSTRY
✔ NUCLEAR ENERGY

Heart-lung Machine

A machine that maintains oxygen in the blood when the heart has stopped

The heart pumps blood around the body, keeping it alive. Surgery on a pumping heart is difficult and dangerous. It is much easier to operate when the heart has stopped. So, a heart-lung machine takes over the heart's job during heart surgery, allowing doctors to stop the heart. Before this machine was first used in 1953, surgeons had just six minutes to operate on a heart before a patient became braindamaged.

HIGHLIGHTS

◆ Before the invention of heart-lung machines, surgeons had only six minutes to operate on a heart before the patient became brain-damaged.

◆ Heart-lung machines maintain oxygen levels in the blood.

◆ The machine also regulates body temperature.

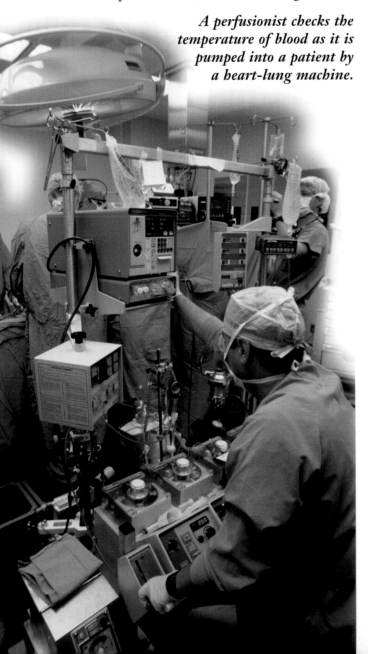

A perfusionist checks the temperature of blood as it is pumped into a patient by a heart-lung machine.

Replacing the heart

The right and left side of the heart are like two pumps that work at the same time. Each side of the heart has two chambers. The upper chambers are called atriums (AY-tree-uhms), the lower ones are ventricles (VEN-tri-kuhls). On each side, the atriums receive blood, and the ventricles pump it out. The right atrium receives blood from the body. This blood is dark red, and it is filled with carbon dioxide gas produced by the body's cells. The right ventricle pumps this blood into the lungs, where carbon dioxide is replaced with oxygen from air that has been breathed in. Oxygen-rich blood reenters the heart, flowing into the left atrium. The left ventricle then pumps this blood back out into the body.

The heart-lung machine bypasses all this. Blood enters the machine through plastic tubes attached to the two very large veins that normally bring blood to the right atrium. Instead, blood flows into the machine's oxygenator (AK-si-jen-ay-tuhr). This part of the machine is underneath the patient, so the blood falls into it. Oxygen gas is bubbled through the blood. The bubbles float the blood up into the part of the machine called the debubbler. Bubbles in the blood can be dangerous to the patient, so the debubbler removes them. Blood clots (solid blood) are also a danger, so these are also removed at this stage.

From the debubbler, oxygen-rich blood trickles through a coiled tube that is inside a bath of water. Doctors can control the temperature of the blood and the patient's body using this water. Often, body temperature is lowered during an operation to slow down the activity of organs and body tissues while the heart has been stopped.

Once the blood is oxygen-rich and ready to be returned to the body, it is pumped through another tube into the aorta (ay-OR-tuh), the main blood vessel leading from the heart. From here, the blood travels around the body before flowing back into the heart-lung machine.

During an operation

Before the heart is stopped, the patient is given a powerful drug called heparin (HEP-uh-rhun). Heparin is an anticoagulant—it stops the blood from clotting. The heart is stopped by clamping

HOW A HEART-LUNG MACHINE WORKS

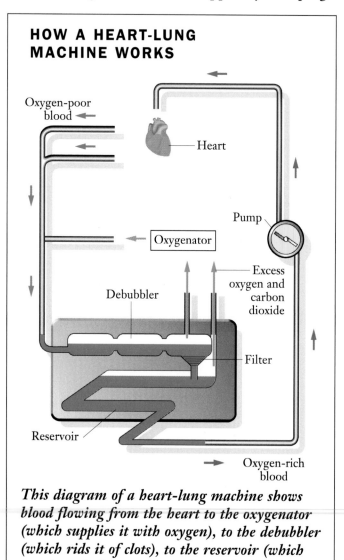

This diagram of a heart-lung machine shows blood flowing from the heart to the oxygenator (which supplies it with oxygen), to the debubbler (which rids it of clots), to the reservoir (which regulates body temperature), and back again.

the aorta to stop blood from flowing out of the heart. As well as maintaining oxygen in the blood and keeping the blood at the correct temperature, the heart-lung machine has connections for drugs. These include drugs that keep the patient unconscious, called anesthetics (a-nuhz-THET-iks), and medicines that lower the activity of the body. Any blood that leaks out of the body through the cuts made by the surgeon is sucked up and added to the blood in the heart-lung machine. This reduces the need to give stored blood to the patient.

During an operation, the heart-lung machine is run by a technician, called a perfusionist, who makes sure the blood being pumped into the patient has the right amount of oxygen and is at the right temperature. A heart-lung machine can be used for several hours. Operations that require a heart-lung machine include heart bypass surgery, surgery on the heart itself, and transplants of the heart and lungs.

Once the operation is over, surgeons restart the heart with an electric shock. Once the heartbeat is strong and regular, the heart-lung machine is turned off and removed from the blood vessels. At this point, a drug is used to restore the clotting action of the patient's blood.

CHECK THESE OUT!

✔MEDICAL TECHNOLOGY ✔SURGERY

Heat Exchanger

A device that transfers heat to or from a liquid or gas

Heat exchangers provide heating and cooling in a wide range of systems. In a refrigerator, a heat exchanger removes heat from the air in the food compartment. It transfers this heat to fluid in its cooling system. The fluid carries the heat to another heat exchanger, which is usually at the back of the refrigerator cabinet. This heat exchanger transfers heat into the surrounding air.

Types of heat exchangers

Heat exchangers transfer heat by passing hot and cold fluids through systems of tubes or plates. Heat always flows from the hot fluid to the cooler one, never the other way around. Several types of heat exchangers are in common use.

HIGHLIGHTS

◆ Heat exchangers remove heat from hot fluids or objects and transfer it to cooler ones.

◆ Double-tube exchangers are the simplest type of heat exchanger.

◆ Shell-and-tube exchangers are most widely used.

The simplest design is the double-tube heat exchanger. This design has two tubes, one inside the other. One fluid flows through the inner tube. The other fluid flows through the space between the two tubes. Heat from the hotter fluid passes into the cooler one.

The most widely used design is the shell-and-tube heat exchanger. This works in the same way as the double-tube heat exchanger. However, instead of a single inner tube, it has a set of many tubes, and instead of an outer tube, it has a cylindrical casing called a shell.

Some heat exchangers use metal plates instead of tubes. In these devices, hot fluid flows through a stack of plates with gaps between them. The plates transfer heat from the hot fluid to the air in these gaps. Some heaters in cars work like this. Hot water from the engine's cooling system passes through the plates.

Uses of heat exchangers

The radiators that cool the engines of cars, motorcycles, and other vehicles are all types of heat exchangers. A household radiator is also a heat exchanger. Computers and other electronic equipment use heat exchangers to keep circuits cool. These exchangers, called heat sinks, are sets of thick aluminum fins fitted onto circuit components. They transfer excess heat to the air, having removed it from the components.

CHECK THESE OUT!
✔HEATING SYSTEMS ✔REFRIGERATION

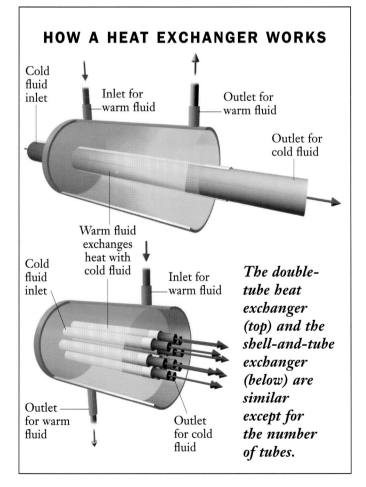

HOW A HEAT EXCHANGER WORKS

Cold fluid inlet

Inlet for warm fluid

Outlet for warm fluid

Outlet for cold fluid

Warm fluid exchanges heat with cold fluid

Cold fluid inlet

Inlet for warm fluid

Outlet for warm fluid

Outlet for cold fluid

The double-tube heat exchanger (top) and the shell-and-tube exchanger (below) are similar except for the number of tubes.

Heating Systems

Devices that produce heat and circulate it through a room or building

No matter how hot or cold the temperature of the surroundings, a well person always has a temperature of about 98°F (37°C). However, humans feel uncomfortable if the temperature falls by more than a certain amount. So, people wear clothes to keep in the heat and keep out the cold. Another way to keep warm is to use heating systems. Ever since the discovery of fire, people have used heating systems to warm the buildings where they live and work.

How heating systems work

All heating systems are based on the same simple idea—making heat in one place and moving it to where it is needed. Heat moves in three different ways: conduction, radiation, and convection.

Conduction is the way heat travels through objects that are touching. If a person touches a heater, heat travels through their fingers by conduction. If they stand some distance from the heater, they can feel the heat it gives off,

Solar panels have been fitted to water tanks to provide hot water for these houses in Israel.

HIGHLIGHTS

♦ Heating systems can be fueled by burning materials such as wood, oil, or coal, or they can be powered directly by electricity.

♦ Heating systems work using a mixture of conduction, radiation, and convection.

♦ In many parts of the world, people use open fires for all their heating and cooking needs.

even though they are not touching it. In this case, heat enters the body by radiation. The heat travels out from the heater as infrared radiation, a type of invisible energy.

The heater also warms the air above it, making it hotter and less dense. As this warm air rises, other air near the ceiling cools and falls back toward the floor. Before long, a kind of up-and-down "conveyor belt" circulates heat through the room, driven by warm, rising air on one side and cool, falling air on the other. This process is called convection and is the third way in which the heater heats a room.

Heating systems work using a mixture of conduction, radiation, and convection. In a wood stove, the burning logs generate heat, which is conducted through the stove. The air warms and begins to circulate around the room by convection. At the same time, the red-hot logs in the stove give off heat directly by radiation.

There are many types of heating systems. Each is suitable for some situations and not for others. Inside a car, people usually want heat to spread within a few minutes of starting the engine. A fan heater is ideal for this. Fan heaters can be expensive to use for long periods, though. Inside the home, it is more economical to use gas-, oil-, or electric-powered radiators.

Direct heating

An open fire is the simplest and oldest type of heating system. It spreads heat mainly by radiation and convection. Sometimes known as direct heating, open fires are the main form of heating for many people around the world. Open fires are usually cheap, burning wood, peat, turf, or coal. However, they produce a great deal of smoke and can be very unhealthy, and it may take some time to gather fuel for an open fire.

An ordinary open fire is often quite inefficient. Lots of wood or other material must be burned to produce enough heat. It is more efficient to burn wood or coal inside a small stove. Inside a stove, higher temperatures are produced and the fuel burns more completely. A chimney provides another improvement. When the smoke and harmful gases produced by burning fuel are taken away, an open fire becomes safer and more pleasant. A chimney also draws in air to the fire, making the material burn more completely.

Central heating

Fires are easy to make, but they do not spread heat very effectively through a building. Large homes were once built with a fireplace and chimney in every room. Laying all the fires, keeping them going, and cleaning the fireplaces was a very tiresome chore.

Central heating solves this problem by generating all the heat needed with a single fire and then spreading the heat efficiently to all parts of the building. Central heating is not a modern

TYPES OF HEATING SYSTEMS

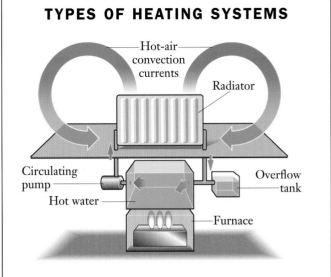

In a hot-water heating system (above), water heated by a furnace circulates through radiators.

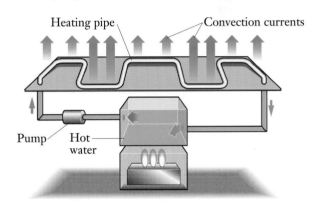

A radiant heat system (above) delivers heat via hot water running along pipes in the floor.

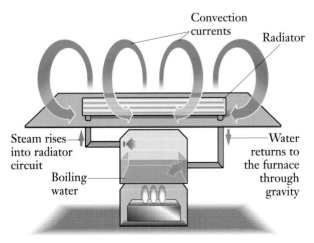

Steam can also be piped to radiators to warm rooms. The steam turns to water as it loses heat.

invention. It was first used by the Romans in their hypocaust heating systems. With the fall of the Roman Empire in the 5th century, the idea was forgotten, but central heating was rediscovered in the early 19th century when people began to warm up large, open factories. Usually, a single coal- or oil-fired furnace in one part of the factory heated a supply of steam that was piped to radiators all around the building. Modern central heating systems have three main parts: a source of heat, a way to move the heat around the building, and a way to control the system automatically. The heat source is usually a hot-water boiler powered by electricity or connected to a furnace that burns wood, coal, oil, or gas. The boiler heats up a supply of water,

LOOK CLOSER

Hypocausts

Central heating was originally invented about 2,000 years ago by the Romans, who built huge furnaces in the basements of some of their buildings. These furnaces, which were usually stoked by slaves, produced constant drafts of warm air that flowed through the columns of brick or concrete that supported the ground floor. A network of ducts carried the hot air through the walls and out through a chimney on the roof. This ingenious heating system was known as a hypocaust, which means "heated from below."

The remains of a Roman hypocaust in Tyre, Lebanon, that heated a bathhouse. Ancient texts suggest that hypocausts may have been invented around the year 80 B.C.E. by a Roman called Sergius Orata, who loved oysters and wanted to cultivate them. He invented a system that provided a constant source of warm water for his oyster beds. This led to the development of the hypocaust.

which is transported as either water or steam around the building to radiators. As these release their heat, the water or steam they carry cools and is returned to the boiler for reheating.

Modern heating systems have automatic controls that switch them on and off at certain times of day. They may also be fitted with thermostats, devices that automatically switch the heating on when the temperature falls below a certain level and then switch it off again once the building has warmed up.

Although central heating systems all work in roughly the same way, they differ in how they transfer the heat. In hot-water heating systems, the boiler heats (but does not boil) water, which is then pumped around each of the radiators in turn. Radiant heating systems are similar, but do not have radiators. Instead, the hot water is pumped through pipes that run under the floor of each room. In a steam central-heating system, the boiler boils the water to produce steam. No pump is required since the high pressure of the steam forces it around the radiators. Forced-air heating is a cross between air conditioning and central heating. The air itself is heated by the furnace and pumped in and out of ducts in each room by large fans.

Heat pumps

Refrigerators continually remove heat from within a sealed compartment and pump it out through a duct to the rear. A type of heating system called a heat pump works rather like a refrigerator in reverse. Heat is taken from outside and drawn into a central compartment. A heat pump uses a device called a heat exchanger, which is fitted on the outside of a building. A pump moves the heat inside. It does not have to be hotter outside the building for a heat pump to function. The atmosphere contains heat that can be transferred inside a building by a heat pump.

District heating

Some parts of the world are blessed with natural heat resources called hot springs. These are sources of hot water that lie underground or may bubble up above the surface. The heat these springs provide is called geothermal energy.

It can be used to warm up buildings and provide them with hot water. Instead of using a furnace, a geothermal heating system takes heat from a hot spring or hot rocks to produce steam. The steam is pumped directly to homes and offices in the local area. Other heating systems are fueled by electricity plants, and some are powered using the heat produced by incinerating trash.

Heat from the Sun

Huge amounts of heat reach Earth every day from the Sun. Even during winter, the Sun delivers enough energy to keep buildings warm, provided they are well designed. Some buildings have large areas of glass that provide a natural heating system, known as passive solar gain. They may also have solar panels on the roof. These panels consist of water pipes sandwiched between sheets of black glass. Heat from the Sun warms up the water in the pipes, which is then pumped inside the building. Energy-efficient buildings like this usually have lots of insulation (heat-trapping material) to keep the heat in. Although these buildings often have conventional central heating systems as well, much of their energy is supplied for free by the Sun.

CHECK THESE OUT!
✔COAL ✔ENERGY RESOURCES ✔SOLAR POWER

LOOK CLOSER

Electric and gas heaters

Electric and gas heaters are usually the quickest ways to heat a room. Gas heaters work by burning a continuous jet of flammable gas either from a bottle or from a domestic supply. Electric heaters were developed in the United States in 1887. Most electric heaters produce heat by passing an electric current through a small coil of wire known as a filament. As the current flows, the filament glows red hot and begins to radiate heat.

Some electric radiators have a number of large filaments called bars. Electric fan heaters blow a continuous gust of cold air across hot filaments to produce a blast of warm air.

Helicopter

An aircraft that uses spinning rotor blades to create lift

Like airplanes, helicopters can move forward, turn left or right, and move up and down. However, helicopters can also fly backward, rotate full circle, and hover motionless in the air.

How helicopters fly

Airplanes can fly because their wings create an upward force called lift. As the airplane moves along, the curved, upper section of the wing makes air travel faster over the top of the wing than under the bottom. This reduces the pressure above the wing and creates the lift force.

A helicopter produces lift with wings called rotor blades. The rotor blades are arranged in a different way from an airplane's wings. Each one is fixed to a structure called the main rotor. Rotor blades produce lift as the main rotor spins on a central shaft. To spin this shaft, the helicopter also needs an engine. As the engine turns the main rotor, the spinning effect of the rotor produces a force called a torque (TORK) on the helicopter body. Torque makes the body spin in the opposite direction to the main

HIGHLIGHTS

◆ The rotor blades of the helicopter's main rotor generate a force called lift, which enables the aircraft to fly.

◆ A helicopter's tail rotor counteracts the force produced as the main rotor rotates.

◆ Turbine engines have increased the reliability and efficiency of the helicopter.

rotor. To stop the helicopter from spinning, another set of rotating wings, called the tail rotor, produces an opposing torque.

Pilot skills

It takes much skill and training to fly a helicopter. The pilot must use both hands and both feet to keep this aircraft in the air. One hand moves the collective control, which adjusts the angle of all the rotor blades at the same time. This action increases or decreases lift to make the helicopter gain or lose height. The other hand moves the cyclic control, which changes the angle of each blade. This allows the helicopter to move forward, backward, left, or right.

A U.S. Chinook helicopter on service during the Vietnam War (1961–1973). This standard troop transporter had a range of 230 miles (360 km).

Foot pedals control the tail rotor, which allows the helicopter to rotate in either direction along the axis of the rotor shaft.

Hovering is an extremely difficult maneuver. The pilot moves both the cyclic control to stay over a fixed point on the ground and the collective controls to stay at the same height. The pilot adjusts the foot pedals to point the helicopter in the same direction.

Overcoming the obstacles

The idea of helicopter travel is not new. Italian artist, engineer, and scientist Leonardo da Vinci (1452–1519), English scientist Sir George Cayley (1773–1857), and U.S. inventor Thomas Edison (1847–1931) laid much of the groundwork. However, these early scientists did not have the technology to put their ideas into practice.

Engineers had to solve many problems before helicopters could take to the skies. They had to answer questions relating to control, materials, power, torque, and vibration. The work of several early pioneers, including French engineer Louis-Charles Breguet (1880–1955), Spanish aeronautical engineer Juan de la Cierva (1896–1936), and German aircraft designer Heinrich Focke (1890–1979), solved many of these individual difficulties.

The first person to look at these problems together was Ukrainian-born U.S. engineer Igor Sikorsky (1889–1972). His logical approach to solving these problems led to the construction of a prototype for the modern helicopter in 1939.

Sikorsky started experimenting with helicopter flight in 1909. For a while, he suspended his investigations and concentrated on conventional aircraft instead. Sikorsky returned to helicopter research in the 1930s, encouraged by the progress of Heinrich Focke, among others. Much of Sikorsky's research focused on a craft called the VS-300. He built this early helicopter from an open framework of metal tubes. In this way, Sikorsky could swap and change the design to try out new ideas and make improvements. Sikorsky kept changing the shape of the VS-300 until he solved the problems that had defeated earlier pioneers. He added a tail rotor to balance torque. He developed control mechanisms so that the helicopter could perform a full range

of movements—up and down, forward and backward, and side to side. He also demonstrated that a helicopter could hover.

The first chopper

The VS-300 led to a range of Sikorsky helicopters, many of which were used in World War II (1939–1945) for jungle rescue and similar missions. The success of Sikorsky's design inspired numerous competitors from different countries. The most famous of these other

HISTORY

Early helicopters

September 1907 Louis-Charles Breguet develops a helicopter with 26-foot-long (7.9 m long) rotors at each end. Breguet's machine becomes the first helicopter to lift itself and a passenger into the air.

November 1907 French engineer Paul Cornu makes the first free (20-second) flight in a helicopter with both one, and then two, passengers.

1909 Igor Sikorsky begins experiments that would lead to the development of the modern helicopter.

1922 A complex helicopter designed by George de Bothezat for the U.S. Army Air Force lifts off the ground for just less than 2 minutes.

1923 Juan de la Cierva makes the first successful flight of his prototype autogiro.

1924 After seven unsuccessful flights, Frenchman Étienne Oehmichen establishes a distance record for helicopters by flying 3,300 feet (1 km).

1936 Heinrich Focke develops the Focke Achegelis Fa 61, which had two three-blade rotors.

1938 German aviator Hanna Reitsch flies the Fa 61 in Berlin to wide acclaim.

1939 Sikorsky starts work on the VS-300, the prototype for the modern helicopter.

The autogiro

In the early 1920s, Juan de la Cierva developed the autogiro. This aircraft looked like an airplane to which a rotor had been added as an afterthought. The autogiro did not have an engine to power the rotor. Rather, the flow of air turned the rotor as the autogiro moved forward. This generated lift at a much lower speed than was possible with conventional aircraft. If the engine propelling the autogiro forward stalled, the rotors would spin so that the autogiro descended to the ground in a controlled way. Cierva also developed the collective control—the mechanism that allows the rotor blades to move up and down and control lift.

designers was U.S. engineer Arthur Young (1905–1995), who had worked on helicopter design for many years. During World War II, Young persuaded a U.S. company, Bell Aircraft Corporation, to fund his research. Like Sikorsky's VS-300, Young's Bell Model 47 worked using a single main rotor and tail. However, Young's rotor had only two rotor blades, where Sikorsky's had five. As the rotor blades turned, they made a chopping sound. This gave Young's model the nickname *chopper*. The bulbous cockpit and open framework of Young's Bell Model 47 soon became familiar throughout the world. Variations of this helicopter were being produced up until the 1970s.

Increasing power

A major problem in helicopter design was engine strength. Even the best piston engines did not give enough power for most helicopters. The invention of the turbine, or jet, engine in 1941, overcame the last major obstacle to the helicopter's success.

Turbines weigh less than comparable piston engines and use cheaper fuel. With a turbine engine, helicopters can fly at much higher speeds and over much greater distances. Increased power output means that helicopters can carry more passengers or cargo. Helicopters soon became efficient carriers. The increased reliability of turbine engines also means safer operations with less risk of disastrous losses of power. Turbine engines produce less vibration than piston engines. This gives a smoother ride and cuts down on expensive maintenance.

Material marvels

The development of new construction materials has made helicopters lighter, safer, and stronger. Modern rotor blades are made from long-lasting plastics rather than from metal. These improvements have made helicopters more economical and more suitable for civilian, rather than just military, use. The helicopter is still a mainstay of the armed forces. Helicopters are used to deploy and retrieve troops, and helicopter gunships are also an extremely useful tool in battle. However, helicopters have many other everyday uses including fire fighting, police work, news reporting, agricultural crop spraying, pest control, medical evacuation, and carrying mail and passengers.

CHECK THESE OUT!
- ✔AERODYNAMICS
- ✔AIRCRAFT DESIGN
- ✔AIRCRAFT ENGINE
- ✔FLIGHT

Igor Sikorsky at the controls of his prototype VS-300 helicopter.

Holography

A method of making three-dimensional pictures using laser light

Photographs provide an important record of the world, but they are not completely accurate. While the human eyes and brain see the full picture of the world in three dimensions, photographs reduce the world to a flat image based on only two dimensions. The invention of holography in 1933 by Hungarian-born British physicist Dennis Gabor (1900–1979) made three-dimensional (3D) images possible. Holography uses laser beams to capture 3D images. These images are called holograms.

What is a hologram?

Because cameras have only one "eye," the photographs they take lack depth. If a person moves his or her head to look at a photograph from a different angle, the image stays exactly the same. Holograms are different. Unlike photographs, they store an accurate 3D picture of the world. As a person moves around in front of a hologram, the image changes as though the hologram were a real object.

A photograph represents how the real world appears to the eye of a camera. In a photograph, the three-dimensional world is "squeezed" into a flat, two-dimensional picture. However, a three-dimensional picture cannot be re-created from a two-dimensional photograph, because all the depth in the original picture is lost when the photograph is taken, and that information can never be recovered.

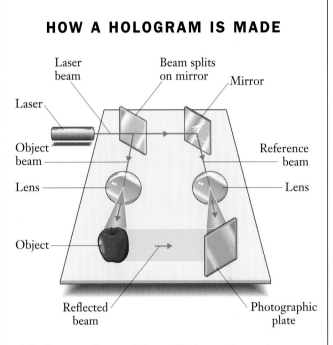

HOW A HOLOGRAM IS MADE

A hologram is made by splitting a laser beam in two and reflecting one of the beams off the object. When the beams are recombined on a photographic plate, interference effects between the light waves create a 3D image.

By contrast, a hologram stores a 3D picture as a pattern of microscopic light and dark lines called fringes. The fringes are not a picture in themselves, but a kind of coded pattern. This pattern records not just the objects in the picture, but how they are arranged in three dimensions. When light shines on a hologram, the pattern is converted back into a three-dimensional picture, like the original object.

How holograms are made

Photographs can be taken in ordinary sunlight or electric light. Holograms can only be made using a much more carefully controlled type of light—the light produced by a laser beam. When a camera takes a photograph, light reflected off the various objects in the scene passes through the lens and makes a pattern on a piece of sensitive film held inside the camera's case. Each tiny individual waves that make up a beam of ordinary light are all jumbled. The crests of one wave travel out at the same time as the troughs of another wave. If a spotlight is shone on an apple to illuminate it for a photograph to be taken, the light waves leaving the spotlight will be jumbled. When the waves hit the apple, and when these waves arrive back at the lens of a camera, they will still be jumbled.

Light from a laser is quite different. All the waves of light that leave a laser are "in step"—all the crests of the waves leave together, followed by all the troughs of the same wave, followed by all the crests of the next wave, and so on. This type of light is called coherent light. When a laser beam hits the apple, some of the waves have to travel farther than others to get around it, so they are slowed down. When the waves finally arrive back at the photographic film, those waves are out of step.

area of the negative of a photograph is either black, white, or a shade of gray somewhere between. A photograph records only the brightness of some part of the original scene. However, each part of a hologram also records information about the position of the various objects in space. This information can be recorded because a laser beam is different from an ordinary beam of light.

An ordinary beam of light consists of many different light waves. Each wave undulates up and down like the waves on the sea. The

In holography, a laser beam is split at its source using a mirror that allows half the beam to travel one way and half another way. One half of the beam, called the object beam, passes around the apple and is then bounced back to meet the original beam, which is called the reference beam. Where the two beams meet, they produce a hologram, a pattern of light and dark fringes. Each point in the hologram contains a record of how much the object beam was disturbed by the apple, compared to the reference beam. This effectively captures a 3D image of the apple that can be viewed again at any time by shining the light from another laser through the hologram.

Types of holograms

Most holograms look quite different from photographs and, unlike photographs, cannot be viewed in ordinary daylight. If a hologram is produced using the two-beam method, it is known as a transmission hologram. This type of hologram can be viewed only if the light from a laser is transmitted or shone straight through it.

Some holograms can be viewed in ordinary light. Known as reflection holograms, they are made by a slightly different process. The reference beam is fired onto the front of a piece of photographic film and the object beam onto the back. Another type of hologram, called a rainbow-transmission hologram, is a type of transmission hologram that can be viewed in normal light. However, it appears to change color when it is viewed from different angles. If one of these holograms is rotated very slowly, the colors seem to pass through all the colors of the rainbow, from red through green to violet.

Uses of holograms

Holograms were once little more than a curiosity. They now have many important industrial and commercial uses. The security marks on credit cards are probably the best-known examples of rainbow-transmission holograms. These are made using a stamp that turns the hologram into a pattern of bumps and grooves on a piece of thin metal foil. Holograms like this are an effective defense against counterfeiters, because it is extremely difficult to copy them.

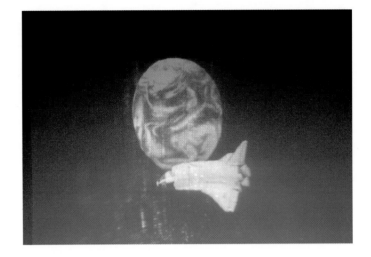

A hologram of the space shuttle orbiting Earth. This moving image was made for film.

Modern fighter pilots often find it difficult to concentrate on both the fast-changing environment outside the cockpit and on the many important instruments inside at the same time. New displays based on holograms help solve this problem. These displays project an image of the instrument panel onto the cockpit window so it is superimposed on the pilot's field of view. Because the pilot no longer has to look up and down, airplanes with this type of display are easier and safer to fly.

CHECK THESE OUT!
✔COMPUTER GRAPHICS ✔MOVIEMAKING
✔PHOTOGRAPHY ✔STORAGE MEDIA

INTO THE FUTURE

Holovideo

Photographs have one big advantage over holograms: they can be run together in a sequence to make a movie. Scientists are trying to find ways to make 3D movies using holograms. One technique called holovideo involves using a computer to calculate the pattern of light and dark fringes that would be produced by an object. The resulting pattern is then displayed on a video screen. The computer can produce many images like this in a rapidly changing sequence, so it effectively produces a continuous 3D "holomovie."

Horticulture

Growing plants for their flowers, fruit, and vegetables

Vegetables were first cultivated in the lands of Mesopotamia (modern Iraq) more than 10,000 years ago. The Romans and ancient Greeks had vineyards and orchards. However, applying plant science to the production of vegetables and fruit for human consumption began less than 400 years ago.

Commercial growers and amateur gardeners grow fruit, vegetables, and mushrooms for food. They also raise ornamental plants for their colorful flowers or sweet smell. These growers usually sell their produce to a distributor, who passes it on to a retail outlet such as a supermarket, grocery store, market, or garden center. Many growers specialize in growing just a small range of plants, depending on the local climate, soil type, or their particular interest.

In recent years, some areas of horticulture have been transformed by advances in technology. Biological science now also plays a role in plant breeding and in the control of pests.

Greenhouse crops

Greenhouses and polyethylene (pah-LEE-ETH-uh-leen) tunnels are now widely used to protect commercially grown plants from wind, frost, rain, and snow. Polyethylene is chosen because it is a lightweight, waterproof material and also a good insulator. Commercial greenhouses may cover a huge area. Inside greenhouses, air temperature and humidity (moisture content) are carefully monitored. Soil moisture is controlled by a system of sprays and pipes above and below the soil. Soil used in commercial greenhouses is often treated to remove weeds and pests. Seedlings are fertilized as necessary and checked for diseases and pests. Pests and diseases may be destroyed using chemical pesticides. Some insect and mollusk pests are controlled through the introduction of natural predators or parasites.

Growing fruit

Commercial fruit growing is big business in many countries, including the United States. Modern fruit farmers usually specialize in

HIGHLIGHTS

◆ Horticulture is the cultivation of plants for their flowers, fruit, or vegetables. Some areas of horticulture have recently been transformed by advances in technology.

◆ Plant breeding aims to produce new, improved strains of plants. Plant breeders select seeds from the best plants in their stock to produce the next generation.

◆ Plant propagation is the controlled reproduction of plants, usually aimed at producing large numbers of existing strains of plants.

growing just a few varieties, to satisfy the demand from supermarkets and the public for unblemished fruit of a particular size, color, and shape. Dwarf species of fruit trees such as apples and pears have recently been developed to make

Tulips being cultivated in the Netherlands, which has the largest bulb fields in the world.

harvesting easier. Modern technology plays a part in many fruit-growing operations. Pest control has now wiped out many of the pests that once infested orchards. However, since most fruit trees are still reared outdoors, trees and fruit can still suffer in bad weather. In spring, heavy rains can damage blossoms, ruining an orchard. Later in the year, high winds can blow fruit from trees.

Growing flowers

Growing flowers on a commercial scale is called floriculture. For centuries, flowers have been grown for their color and scent. More recently, they have also been grown for oils used to make perfumes. Some growers specialize in producing seeds and developing new varieties of particular flowering plants, such as roses and tulips.

Flowers may be grown commercially in greenhouses or in the open. The tulip fields of the Netherlands and the rose fields of Zimbabwe are examples of commercial flower growing that takes place outdoors.

Plant breeding

Plant breeding and propagation are vital to the success of both horticulture and farming. Propagation is the controlled reproduction of plants, usually with the aim of increasing plant numbers. While plant breeders aim to improve particular strains of plants, the purpose of propagation is usually to produce large numbers of existing types of plants.

Plant breeding

Plants have been grown for food in the Middle East for at least 10,000 years. Early farmers began to cultivate food crops by collecting seeds from edible wild plants and sowing them the following year. Seeds from the best plants with the highest yields would be saved. Over many years, wild plants gradually developed into the modern high-yield strains.

Plant breeders still work to increase the yield or grain size of crop plants and the color and scent of garden plants. New strains of plants are developed to withstand frost or high temperatures, or to resist disease. Commercial breeders protect new plants that they have developed from being grown by other gardeners by gaining official licenses called patents.

Modern growers still begin the breeding process by selecting seeds from plants that display the most desirable qualities. They carefully assess the first generation of plants that sprout from the seed, called the F1 generation, to make sure that the plants that have been selected for breeding have all the right qualities.

Breeders use different techniques that depend on the plant's natural method of reproduction. Some plants reproduce by self-pollination—they

Hydroponics

LOOK CLOSER

Hydroponics is the technique of cultivating plants in nutrient-rich water instead of soil. The plants are usually suspended in a tank of water that contains a carefully controlled mixture of nutrients (nourishing minerals). Alternatively, they are grown in a support medium, such as gravel or processed mineral fibers, known as rock wool. Hydroponics is often used in areas where the soil is poor or space is limited, for example, in cities. Plants reared using hydroponics can be grown very close together. They also require less water than plants grown by conventional methods, so hydroponics is used in dry regions. Hydroponic plants are usually grown under cover in a greenhouse, such as the one below.

Pollination

Many of the world's most important food crops, including cereals, reproduce by self-pollination. These so-called inbreeding plants tend to "breed true" for many generations—that is, they produce offspring very similar to themselves. Breeders who wish to develop new strains of self-pollinating plants must introduce new genetic material artificially. This is done by artificial cross-pollination. Breeders physically remove the male parts from all the flowers on one plant, before they have shed their pollen, to form an all-female plant. Pollen from another carefully selected plant is then placed on the female plant's flowers. Fertilization takes place, resulting in hybrid or cross-bred plants.

Cross-pollinating plants include many vegetables. These plants never naturally breed true. Instead, they produce a wide range of types from which growers can choose to breed. Sometimes, cross-breeding plants are made to inbreed by artificial self-pollination. Two strains developed in this way can then be cross-bred to form a hybrid strain.

The production of hybrid strains, called hybridization, is important in plant breeding. Hybrids are generally strong and hardy because they contain genetic material from both their parents. High-yielding hybrid varieties are now used by many growers. The disadvantage is that growers need to buy new seed each year, because hybrid plants produce very variable offspring.

Growing plants from seed

Plants may be propagated (bred) either sexually, which means growing them from seed, or asexually, by taking cuttings or using other methods. Growing plants from seed is cheap and allows plants to be stored in seed form for years if necessary. Seed is easy to transport and resistant to disease. However, plants grown from seed can be different from their parents.

Seed production is a specialized area of horticulture. Growers aim to produce the maximum number of healthy seeds that will grow into plants of a predictable type. Some seeds require treatment before they will germinate (sprout), such as being exposed to freezing temperatures or soaked in water.

fertilize themselves with their own pollen. Others are cross-pollinators. They are fertilized by pollen from a different plant of the same species.

Asexual propagation

Some plants can reproduce asexually without need for pollination. One of the advantages of this is that the offspring are genetically identical to their parents. Asexual propagation is also often faster than growing plants from seed. Methods of asexual propagation include dividing root systems, taking cuttings, layering, grafting, and growing plants from runners, tubers, or bulbs.

Cut portions of stem, leaf, or root can often be made to develop into whole new plants. Leaf and root cuttings develop in this way when placed in compost. Stem cuttings are dipped in a powder that encourages them to root. This hormone rooting powder is applied before the cuttings are placed in compost.

In layering, the plant stem is "wounded" (cut slightly) and then pegged down in the soil. Roots develop from the wound, then the stem is cut to form a new plant. Alternatively, a ball of moist growing medium is placed around the stem.

Grafting involves physically joining two closely related plants. One of the plants is cut, and the shoot of the other plant is inserted into the cut. The two cut surfaces form wound tissue and eventually fuse together. This technique is commonly used with roses.

Many vegetable plants, such as potatoes, carrots, and onions, produce tubers or bulbs from which the plants sprout. Other plants, such as strawberries, reproduce by growing runners that develop into new plants, which makes their propagation easy.

Specialty crops

Specialty crops are an increasingly popular area of horticulture. Growers choose to grow an unusual crop either because they have a personal interest in the plant or because they see a growing market for it. Examples include bok choy, which is grown mainly for Asian cuisine, and herbs for cooking and aromatherapy.

CHECK THESE OUT!
✔CROP FARMING ✔GENETIC ENGINEERING

These wild sea oats, which are used to help prevent beach erosion, are being grown in a tunnel as a speciality crop.

Household Appliances

Devices that save time and labor in domestic chores

Before household appliances became common, leisure time was for the rich only. Ordinary people spent much of their time washing their clothes, scrubbing floors, or preparing food. This situation began to change slowly in the 19th century. With the invention of the first hot-water central heating system in 1840, some households gradually replaced their open fires. Gas stoves appeared in 1826. Electric stoves, however, were not developed until the late 1880s.

The mechanical washing machines invented in the 1860s took some of the effort out of keeping clothes clean. However, it took another 50 years before the electric washing machine finally allowed wealthier people to hand the whole job over to a machine. The first carpet cleaners appeared in the United States in 1905, but it was many years before they became widespread. Refrigerator-freezers appeared in the United States around 1910. Before that, cold food had to be kept in a wooden box, to which several large chunks of ice had to be added each week.

These bigger machines catered to household essentials such as keeping clean and warm. However, a number of smaller appliances are just as important to modern households. Irons, sewing machines, microwave ovens, and food processors all make people's lives easier and leave them with more time for leisure pursuits.

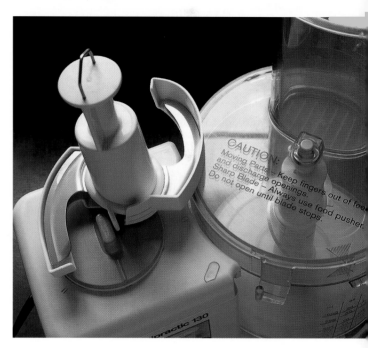

The food processor is now commonplace but was invented, in France, as recently as 1971.

All these appliances were expensive when they were first introduced. It took until the second half of the 20th century before most household appliances were cheap enough for the average household in Europe or North America.

Irons

The first irons were blocks of iron with a flat bottom and a handle on top. The block was heated over a fire, or later a gas ring, to make it hot enough to press creases out of clothes. By the 19th century, it was possible to pour molten iron into a cast to create a hollow iron. These irons had an internal space that could be filled with hot water or with another slab of iron called a billet. The billet was heated instead of the iron. Using a billet, people did not have to stop ironing every time the iron cooled down. They could simply swap a cool billet for a hot one.

Metal irons had no temperature control. Synthetic fibers, such as nylon, can melt or scorch at lower temperatures than wool or cotton. Luckily, by the time that nylon was

HIGHLIGHTS

♦ Machines invented in the 19th century gave people much more free time.

♦ Before the invention of electric irons, metal blocks for pressing clothes were heated over open fires.

♦ Many household appliances of the future will be controlled by computers.

PEOPLE

Elias Howe

French tailor Barthelemy Thimmonier (1793–1859) produced a basic sewing machine in the 1830s, but his machines were destroyed by rioting tailors who feared they would be put out of business. In 1841, U.S. textile worker Elias Howe (1819–1867) made a more advanced practical sewing machine. In Howe's design, a thread was passed through a needle that carried the cotton down through the fabric. Here, it was wound around a second thread before the needle raised up to take the next stitch. Although he took out a patent, Howe was unsuccessful in promoting his machine. He went to England, where he was swindled out of his royalties. Returning to the United States in poverty, he found that other inventors had adapted his ideas. After years of legal battles, Howe eventually earned back royalties from his rivals.

invented in 1935, electric irons were already on the market. These are fitted with a temperature control for different materials.

Smaller appliances

The earliest electric motors were large and cumbersome. As designers slowly reduced the weight and complexity of motors, a new generation of household appliances appeared in the middle of the 20th century.

Food processors and electric mixers take the hard work out of combining ingredients for a cake or squeezing oranges for juice. The first food processors had a motor mounted over a mixing bowl. The appliance came with a number of different beaters for various purposes such as kneading

Microwave ovens are now compact. The first ones, in 1954, were as large as a refrigerator.

dough for bread or whisking egg whites. Food processors became more popular after they were fitted with smaller motors and plastic casings. In modern times, very compact machines are available to chop and slice vegetables, grate cheese, and mix ingredients.

Many smaller personal household appliances are taken for granted but have been widely available for less than half a century. Hair driers shoot a jet of air over a heating element. Early versions were large and inconvenient. Driers only became common when they could be handheld with ease. The electric toothbrush is a more recent invention. It has a small motor to power a disposable brush that twists and turns to clean between the teeth. Electric razors are fitted with a thin layer of pierced metal foil to protect the skin from the cutters behind.

Household appliances of the future are likely to be smaller still. Computer technology may take over tasks such as turning lamps on and off. "Smart" automated vacuum cleaners are already available. The dream of using robots to carry out every household chore is still a long way away, but technology has advanced enough to make most domestic work much easier.

CHECK THESE OUT!

✔STOVES AND OVENS ✔VACUUM CLEANER ✔WASHING MACHINE AND DISHWASHER

Hovercraft

Vehicles that travel on cushions of air

A hovercraft, or air-cushion vehicle (ACV), is a boatlike vehicle that flies just above the ground. It creates a layer of pressurized air below its hull. This layer, or cushion, of air lifts the craft clear of the surface beneath it. Hovercraft have one or more propellers like those on an aircraft. These drive the hovercraft forward. Hovercraft can travel rapidly over any flat surface such as water, land, ice, or swamp.

The hovercraft was invented by English engineer Christopher Cockerell (1910–1999). Cockerell, an electronics engineer, had planned to spend his retirement as a boat builder, but had become fascinated by the challenge of building a craft that traveled on a cushion of air. He patented his invention in 1955, and the world's first practical hovercraft, the SR-N1, was

HOW A HOVERCRAFT WORKS

A hovercraft uses a fan to suck air into the area between the craft and the ground to create a cushion of air. This cushion inflates the flexible skirt and lifts the craft off the ground.

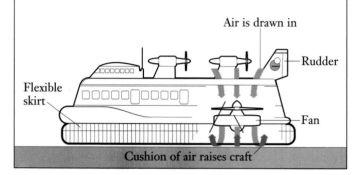

Air is drawn in

Rudder

Flexible skirt

Fan

Cushion of air raises craft

based on his design. In 1959, it made its first journey over open water, from the Isle of Wight to the English mainland. A few weeks later, it crossed the English Channel from England to France.

Hovercraft in service

In the 1960s, companies in the United States, France, and Japan, as well as in Britain, made hovercraft. Most were used as ferries. However, by the 1970s, interest in hovercraft faded because they are expensive to run and cannot operate safely in strong winds and high waves. Many ferry operators who had introduced hovercraft replaced them with high-speed hydrofoil boats. The hovercraft service between England and France, for example, has been discontinued. Despite these problems, the most important use for hovercraft is still ferrying people and cars across relatively short stretches of water. They are much faster than ordinary ferries and can come ashore to load and unload.

Because they can travel over both land and water, the military forces of many countries still use hovercraft to land troops and fighting vehicles on enemy shores. Hovercraft are also useful in areas such as marshland and

LOOK CLOSER

Military uses of hovercraft

During the Vietnam War (1961–1973), the U.S. Army patrolled rivers, marshland, and rice fields with hovercraft. These craft were especially useful for operations on the waterlogged land of the Mekong Delta in southern Vietnam. The military also use hovercraft to ferry troops and equipment ashore from amphibious assault ships. The U.S. Navy operates more than 80 LCAC-1 hovercraft. The LCAC-1 is 88 feet (26 m) long and 47 feet (14.3 m) wide. Two of its four gas turbine engines drive its two propellers, and the other two drive its four lift fans. Launched from an assault ship up to 50 miles (80 km) offshore, an LCAC-1 can carry a load of up to 75 tons (68 metric tons) at a speed of 46 miles per hour (74 km/h). The first major combat deployment of LCAC-1s was in the Gulf War of 1991. Some of the largest military hovercraft now in use are the Pormornik (Zubr) hovercraft built in Russia and Ukraine. These are each capable of carrying ten armored personnel carriers and 230 troops. They have a top speed of 70 miles per hour (113 km/h).

This hovercraft can skim over water and reeds.

sandy deserts where conventional wheeled or tracked vehicles would sink into the soft ground. Some rescue services also use hovercraft to save people who have fallen through ice.

How hovercraft work

In the basic hovercraft design, a large fan (the lift fan) blows air down through an opening in the bottom of the hull. A flexible rubber skirt running all around the outside edge of the hull traps this air underneath the hull. The space between the hull and the ground, and enclosed by the skirt, is called the plenum. The air

pressure in the plenum increases, and the air lifts the hull up clear of the ground. Depending on the size of the hovercraft, the hull rises between 6 inches (15 cm) and 9 feet (2.7 m) above the ground. When the hull is lifted clear of the ground, some air escapes from under the skirt. However, this air is replaced by air that is pumped in from above to maintain the cushion of air in the plenum. As long as the lift fan is blowing air into the plenum, the hovercraft will float on its cushion of air. With the hull no longer in contact with the ground or water, it is easy for the propeller to drive the craft forward.

To increase the lifting power of the air cushion, most modern hovercraft blow the air down in a narrow stream around the inside edge of the hull. This stream of air creates a curtain of high-pressure air around the outside of the plenum. The combination of this air curtain and the flexible skirt increases the air pressure in the plenum.

Small hovercraft use a single gasoline or diesel engine to drive both the lift fan and the propeller. Larger craft must have separate gas turbine engines for the fans and propellers.

Because they float clear of the surface, hovercraft cannot use wheels or underwater rudders to steer. Instead, they swivel their propellers to change direction. Many also have tail fins with rudders like those on aircraft. To help them slow down and stop, and to move backward, hovercraft reverse the action of the propeller blades. This allows the blades to push the craft backward instead of forward.

HIGHLIGHTS

◆ A hovercraft is a propeller-driven vehicle that floats on a cushion of trapped air.

◆ Hovercraft steer by swiveling their propellers.

◆ Christopher Cockerell patented the first practical hovercraft design in 1955.

CHECK THESE OUT!
✔AERODYNAMICS ✔SHIP AND BOAT

Hydraulics

Controlling machines by the use of liquids under pressure

Long before people understood how to harness electricity, they used the movement of fluids such as water and oil to drive machinery and to transmit forces from one place to another. Machines that operate using the movement of liquids are known as hydraulic (hy-DRAW-lik). The main modern day uses of hydraulics are in heavy lifting equipment, in vehicle transmissions (drive systems), and brakes.

How hydraulics works

A gas takes up less space when pressure is applied to it. However, liquids shrink only a very small amount. Because a liquid under pressure cannot be compressed significantly, it will flow from one place to another if it is free to move. This principle lies behind all hydraulic systems.

The principle can be demonstrated with a large drum full of oil. Imagine the drum is sealed at the top except for two open pipes sticking out. Two metal rods fit snugly into the pipes. If one of the rods is pushed down one of the pipes, the other rod rises by an equal amount. As pressure is increased down one of the pipes, it pushes oil down into the drum. However, the oil cannot be compressed inside, so it must rise up out of the other pipe, pushing the rod up as it does so.

If one of the pipes is much narrower, and force is applied down the wider pipe, the liquid will rise much higher up the narrow pipe. This is the basic mechanism inside a hydraulic jack. In a wide pipe, a fairly small force is applied to a liquid when, for example, a person pumps up and down on a handle. This action would produce a much greater force in a narrow pipe—so great that it would be capable of lifting a car or a truck right up off the ground.

Hydraulic systems

Many hydraulic systems are more complex than a simple hydraulic jack. Mechanical excavators, for example, usually have hydraulic buckets or claws at either end. Hydraulic power is produced not by a person pumping on a handle but by a diesel engine driving a hydraulic pump. This action drives oil into or out of the hydraulic rams connected to the bucket, causing them to rise up or lower down to the ground.

Hydraulic systems contain motors that are rotated by the pressure of fluid. Unlike electric motors, there is no risk of hydraulic motors producing sparks, so they are safer to operate in places where there are flammable chemicals.

Hydraulic circuits

Just as electric components such as lamps and batteries can be connected together into circuits, so hydraulic components can be linked together to make hydraulic circuits. A flowing fluid

HIGHLIGHTS

◆ Hydraulic systems use water or liquid to operate machines.

◆ Hydraulics is based on the fact that a liquid cannot be compressed.

◆ Pneumatics is similar to hydraulics but uses compressed air rather than a fluid.

HYDRAULIC DRUM BRAKES

Pressing on a car brake pedal pushes a piston into the master cylinder. Hydraulic fluid transmits the pressure to pistons in each wheel's slave cylinder. In drum brakes, pistons force brake shoes against the brake drum, slowing the car. In disk brakes, the pistons make pads grip the disk.

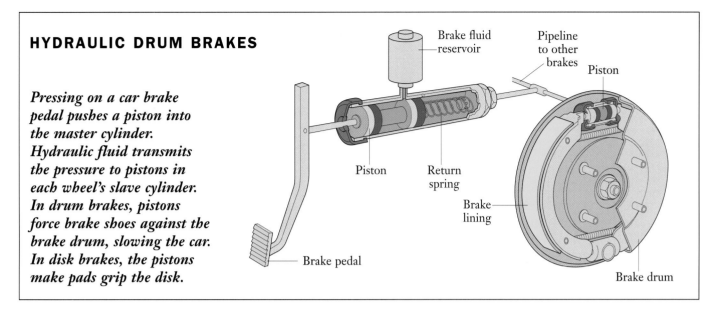

drives a hydraulic current. The components in a hydraulic circuit are also quite similar to the components in an electric circuit. In an electric circuit, a battery provides a constant source of current. In a hydraulic circuit, a reservoir provides a constant source of fluid. Some modern hydraulic circuits include the ability to turn hydraulic devices on and off automatically.

Fluid Drive

The transmission in an automobile connects the vehicle's engine to the wheels that drive it along using gear wheels. Depending on the road conditions, the gears either increase the speed or the power with which the driving wheels turn. In many cars, the driver has to change gears manually by moving the gearshift. In a car with automatic transmission, the gears are changed using hydraulics inside a fluid drive.

In a fluid drive, a shaft connected to the engine and a shaft connected to the driving wheels are fixed inside a

This Ford dump truck transports bulky material. A hydraulic system is used to tilt the body of the truck, dumping out the contents.

fluid-filled chamber. Each has a windmill-like wheel called a turbine at one end. As the engine shaft turns, it makes the fluid inside the chamber churn around. This causes the drive shaft to turn, too. If the driver presses down on the gas pedal, the engine turns over faster. The engine shaft spins more quickly, churning the fluid around faster and pushing the drive shaft faster, too. In a fluid drive, the hydraulic fluid acts like a "liquid gear," linking the two shafts together.

Most commonly used in cars and trucks, hydraulics have many industrial and other applications, particularly in braking systems.

CHECK THESE OUT!

✔AUTOMOBILE ✔AUTOMOBILE STEERING
✔AUTOMOBILE SUSPENSION ✔BRAKE SYSTEMS

LOOK CLOSER

Pneumatics

Pneumatic (noo-MAT-ik) systems are quite similar to hydraulic ones, except they use compressed air as the controlling fluid instead of oil or water. Because air is lighter and easier to channel through pipes, pneumatic systems are generally more portable than hydraulic ones. Highway drills are powered by pneumatics, not by hydraulics. However, heavy-duty machinery uses hydraulics, because it can be up to 50 times more powerful than pneumatics.

Hydroelectricity

**Electricity generated by
the power of flowing water**

In a hydroelectric (hydro) power plant, fast-flowing water from a river, or a lake behind a dam, turn blades in turbines. Turbines drive generators that produce electricity. Because they are powered by river water, hydro plants produce no pollution and are a renewable energy source.

The first hydroelectric plant in the United States was a small unit on the Fox River at Appleton, Wisconsin. It started operation in 1882 and produced 125 kilowatts (kW) of electricity. Soon, power companies across the United States built hydroelectric plants. By the 1940s, these plants produced 40 percent of the nation's electrical power.

After World War II (1939–1945), the demand for hydroelectricity fell. Most new power plants in the 1950s and 1960s generated power by

HIGHLIGHTS

◆ In a hydroelectric plant, powerful flows of water turn turbines that drive electricity generators.

◆ Hydroelectricity is the source of around 20 percent of the world's electrical power.

◆ A hydroelectric plant creates no pollution, but it can cause other environmental problems.

burning fossil fuels—coal, oil, and natural gas. These plants were less expensive to build than hydroelectric plants, and fossil fuels were cheap. Hydroelectricity now provides around 10 percent of the electrical power in the United States and around 20 percent of electricity worldwide.

Harnessing a river

At a typical hydroelectric plant, a dam built across a river in a deep valley or gorge holds back the water. This creates a deep artificial lake called a reservoir, penned in by the dam and the valley

Built in the 1960s, the Aswan Dam, on the Nile River, doubled the electricity supply of Egypt.

sides. Inside the dam, water from the reservoir flows through large pipes called penstocks. This flow has great force. At the bottom of each penstock, the water flows past a turbine, a large horizontal wheel with curved blades around its edge. Water pushes against the blades and turns the turbine at a speed of around 90 rpm (revolutions per minute). The rotating turbine turns a shaft that drives an electricity generator. From the turbine, water flows through an outlet pipe and into the river downstream of the dam.

A pumped storage hydro plant has two reservoirs, one above the plant and the other below it. To produce electricity, water from the upper reservoir flows down to the plant and drives its turbines. Then, the water flows into the lower reservoir. At night, when the demand for electricity is low, the plant pumps water from the lower reservoir back up into the upper one, to be used again.

A large hydroelectric plant can produce thousands of megawatts (millions of watts) of power each day. Although most of the world's hydroelectricity comes from large plants, there are also many smaller plants in use. Most of the small plants store little or no water. Some have

Turbines at the Ardnacrusha hydro plant in Ireland.

small dams just a few feet high, while others simply channel the river water through their turbines. The power outputs of these small plants range from just a few kilowatts (thousands of watts)—enough for an individual home or farm—to several megawatts or more.

Power from water

If all the rivers and streams in the world could be used for hydroelectricity, they would supply the world's power needs comfortably. This is not possible for a number of reasons. In some areas, rivers flow across flat land that has no deep valleys in which to build dams. In others, rivers carry little water in the drier parts of the year. Some areas that would be good places to build plants are too remote, and it would cost too much to build and operate them there.

Hydroelectricity is a clean and renewable energy source, but it has some drawbacks. It takes around ten years to plan and build a hydro plant. Constructing dams is usually very expensive. Damming rivers can also damage the environment. The lake behind a dam can cover important wildlife habitats, archeological sites, farmland, and even entire towns and villages.

LOOK CLOSER

The Grand Coulee Dam

The Grand Coulee Dam on the Columbia River, Washington, is the largest hydroelectric plant in the United States. It is also the largest concrete structure ever built. The Franklin D. Roosevelt Lake, created behind the dam, is 150 miles (240 km) long, and its water level is 350 feet (105 m) above the original riverbed. Construction of the dam began in 1933. It started producing electricity in 1942, with two power plants. A third power plant, added in the 1970s, brought the total number of turbines in the three plants to 24. Each turbine is fed by its own penstock, and each penstock is up to 40 feet (12 m) across. The Grand Coulee facility can produce around 7 million kilowatts of electricity. The reservoir also provides irrigation for more than half a million acres (202,000 hectares) of arid land.

CHECK THESE OUT!
✔DAM ✔ELECTRICITY ✔ENERGY RESOURCES

Hydrofoil

A high-speed boat held above the surface of water by lift

Hydrofoils are boats that use wings to travel over water instead of through it. Normally, the resistance of water, known as drag, slows a boat down. However, a hydrofoil's underwater wings, called its foils, lift it out of the water and above the waves. This allows it to travel at much greater speeds. The first hydrofoil was produced in 1918 by U.S. inventor Alexander Graham Bell (1847–1922). Hydrofoils are widely used now as fast passenger ferries and military vessels.

When an airplane flies through the sky, air travels faster over the top of its wings than under the bottom. This reduces the air pressure above the wings and pushes them upward. This upward

HIGHLIGHTS

◆ Hydrofoils have wings (foils) that lift their hulls above the waves.

◆ Seagoing hydrofoils have foils that are submerged beneath the water.

◆ Hydrofoils that operate in coastal waters have foils that skim like waterskis.

force, called lift, holds the airplane up in the sky. Hydrofoils work in much the same way, only their wings are submerged under the water. When a hydrofoil first starts moving, the hull (main compartment) of the boat drags slowly through the water. As it picks up speed, its foils produce lift that slowly raises the hull upward. At higher speeds, the hull lifts out of the water completely, cutting drag to a minimum.

HYDROFOIL MOTION OVER WAVES

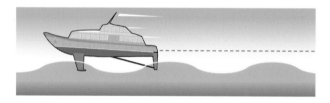

Platforming: When waves are small, the craft remains at a constant level.

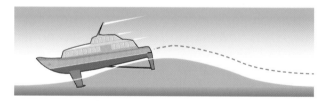

Contouring: When waves are large, the craft follows the contours of the surface.

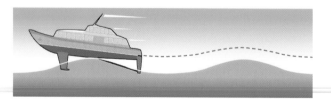

Intermediate response: The hydrofoil follows a smoothed path in intermediate conditions.

Command and control

Most hydrofoils have a large foil on either side of the hull, near the front, to provide lift. There is usually also a smaller foil near the back to control side-to-side movement, which is called the attitude. Hydrofoils designed to travel out at sea, where waves are large, have different foils from those that travel near the coast.

Hydrofoils that travel in coastal waters typically have foils that pierce the surface of the water. Boats rise up on these foils and eventually skim across the surface of the water like a person on waterskis. In rougher waters out at sea, these foils would exaggerate the motion of the waves and make it difficult to control the boat. For this reason, seagoing hydrofoils have submerged foils that travel beneath the water and do not rise up to the surface. Unlike surface-piercing foils, submerged foils help reduce pitching, the up-and-down movement caused by waves. This makes the boat easier to control and gives a smoother ride for the passengers.

Hydrofoils travel in different ways, depending on the size of the waves. Because waves generally affect only the surface of the ocean, a hydrofoil can smooth out a choppy sea if it rides with its foils beneath the waves and its hull above them. Known as platforming, this offers the passengers a particularly smooth ride. When the waves are much larger, in rougher seas, a hydrofoil cannot smooth out the up-and-down motion of the waves and, instead, the hydrofoil has to follow their contours just like a normal boat.

Hydrofoil power

Hydrofoils need powerful engines to accelerate quickly to the speed at which the foils can be effective. Some hydrofoils have high-speed diesel engines; others have even more powerful gas-turbine engines similar to those used in airplanes. Not all hydrofoils have conventional engines. Jetfoils are powered by huge jets of water that squirt backward to push the hull forward.

Hydrofoils suffer a problem called cavitation. At high speeds, tiny bubbles form and burst around the tops of the foils as they cut through the water. Apart from causing a bumpy ride, cavitation gradually eats away the surface of the foils. This reduces their effectiveness. The problem is usually solved by pumping air down to the foils to prevent cavitation bubbles from forming.

Hydrofoils at work

In many parts of the world, hydrofoils are used as high-speed ferries, especially where

LOOK CLOSER

Military hydrofoils

In the early 1960s, the U.S. Navy commissioned a high-performance hydrofoil gunboat, the Grumman Flagstaff. It carried a 6-inch (152 mm) gun from a Sheridan tank on its deck. Its hydrofoil design gave it a number of advantages. Once its hugely powerful Rolls Royce gas turbine engine had lifted it out of the water, this hydrofoil could reach a top speed of 40 knots (74 km/h). Because it traveled over the water, instead of through it, the Grumman Flagstaff could withstand explosions from mines that would have sunk a normal gunboat.

traveling across the bay of a city can be much faster than making the same journey over land. In countries such as Norway, Japan, and Italy, high-speed, low-cost hydrofoils compete with airplanes for short-haul travel.

Elsewhere, the smooth ride and much-reduced journey times offered by hydrofoils have made them a popular choice for car and passenger ferries. The speedy response of hydrofoils has also made them very popular as military attack and coast guard patrol boats. They have been widely used in the fight against drug smuggling off the coast of California.

CHECK THESE OUT!
✔FLIGHT ✔HOVERCRAFT
✔SHIP AND BOAT

A jetfoil (left) and a hydrofoil carrying passengers in Hong Kong harbor.

Ignition System

Systems that enable fuel mixtures to ignite safely

Engines work by converting energy from a burning mixture of fuel and air into movement. This burning reaction is made possible by ignition (ig-NI-shuhn; catching fire). In engines, ignition takes place inside small chambers called cylinders.

Inside an engine

The engines of most automobiles have four cylinders. Inside each cylinder, a piston moves up and down. First, the piston moves down to suck in fuel and air. Then, the piston pushes up and squeezes the mixture. When the piston has pushed the fuel to the top of each cylinder, the ignition system ignites the fuel mixture. The system's timing ensures that the fuel mixture catches fire at exactly this point. The force of the resulting explosion pushes the piston down again. As the piston moves up again, it blows out the burned gases. A connecting rod attached to each piston turns metal joints attached to part of the engine called the crankshaft. As the pistons move up and down, the rods turn the crankshaft around. This, in turn, makes the wheels spin.

Compression ignition

Compression ignition works by injecting fuel into air so hot that the fuel ignites instantly. The high temperatures required for compression ignition occur when air is compressed in the cylinder. The timing and the amount of fuel that is injected into the compressed air is controlled precisely. Compression-ignition systems are more expensive than spark-ignition systems. The engines are also noisier and heavier. Diesel engines, which operate through compression ignition, are also harder to start in cold weather.

HIGHLIGHTS

- An engine uses an ignition system to ignite a mixture of fuel and air.

- Gasoline-powered engines work by spark ignition.

- Diesel engines work using compression ignition.

There are three main ignition systems: hot-tube, spark-, and compression-ignition. The hot-tube system was developed first, then came the spark-ignition system. The compression-ignition system is the most modern.

Hot-tube ignition

Hot-tube ignition works by heating a metal tube until it is red-hot before the engine starts. Once the engine is running, the heat of the burning fuel keeps the tube hot. The fuel mixture ignites when it touches the hot tube. The timing of hot-tube ignition is set at a constant rate, so it works best for stationary engines that run at a low, constant speed. Hot-tube ignition is not suitable for automobile engines, but it is used in pumps and other industrial machinery.

Spark ignition

Gasoline-powered engines use an electric spark to ignite the compressed fuel mixture. Spark ignition was developed to allow an automobile engine to run smoothly at different speeds. Spark ignition requires an external source of power. An automobile's electrical power is stored in the battery. Electrical current from the battery first flows to an ignition coil, which converts low-voltage electricity (12 V) from the battery into high-voltage electricity (more than 40,000 V).

The ignition coil is the heart of the ignition system. As current flows through the ignition coil, a strong magnetic field builds up. When the current shuts off, the collapse of the magnetic field generates a high voltage in the coil. The high-voltage current passes into a device called a distributor, which transmits electricity through ignition wires. The distributor has one wire going into its center from the ignition coil. The number of ignition wires depends on the number of cylinders: four, six, or eight. These wires come out of the distributor and send the high voltage to a spark plug at the top of each cylinder.

The spark plug contains a break in the electrical wires, but the voltage is so high that electricity jumps the gap. This produces a spark of electricity that ignites the mixture of fuel and air. Spark ignition is timed so that only one cylinder receives a spark from the distributor at any one time. The engine camshaft operates the ignition timing. The camshaft opens and closes the inlet and the exhaust valves that are fitted at the top of each cylinder. The exhaust valve opens to allow the waste gases to escape into the automobile's exhaust system. The spark plug is timed to spark when both valves have closed both holes.

Drivers worked the earliest spark-ignition systems using a hand-operated lever. This was inconvenient, so automatic methods developed using a system of weights and levers to time the spark in each cylinder. Computer technology has led to electronic timing mechanisms. These systems control the timing using a computerized sensor on the crankshaft. Electronic control is much more accurate than mechanical timing.

Impurities in the fuel mixture may mean that it will not burn completely. If the spark occurs too early or too late in the cycle, the fuel mixture will not ignite at the right time. If the timing is wrong, the engine will run but it will not deliver full power. If ignition occurs well before it should, a condition called knocking occurs. In this case, the cylinder tries to stop the engine and may seriously damage it. Knocking may also occur if the wrong fuel is put into the engine.

CHECK THESE OUT!
✔AUTOMOBILE ✔ENGINE

COMPUTERIZED IGNITION SYSTEM

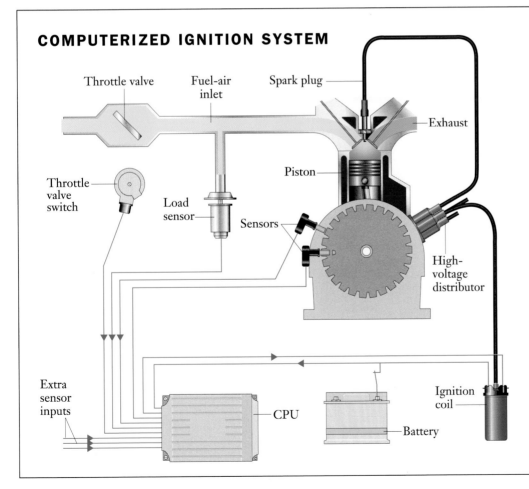

In many vehicles, a computerized system has taken over the timing of the ignition of the mixture of fuel and air. This ensures that ignition is very precisely controlled. Sensors are located throughout the ignition system to measure the speed, load, temperature, and air pressure of the engine. Sensors also indicate the position of the crankshaft. All this information is fed back to the central processing unit (CPU), which ignites the spark plugs at the correct moment.

Immunology

The study of the body's defenses against disease

Diseases are caused by tiny microorganisms, such as bacteria, and viruses that infect the body. As they multiply, these disease-causing agents, or pathogens (PATH-uh-juhns), affect the way the body works, causing disease symptoms. Animals, including people, fight pathogens using their natural defenses, the immune system.

Battle in the blood

There are three main types of blood cells traveling through the body. Red blood cells carry oxygen from the lungs to the body's tissues, while platelets are cell fragments that help blood clot, forming scabs that keep pathogens out of wounds. White blood cells are an essential part of the immune system, protecting the body against infection. The immune system's first line of defense is the skin. White blood cells called phagocytes (FAG-uh-syts), which travel around the body in search

of pathogens, are the second line of defense. When these cells come into contact with a pathogen, they engulf it and break it up into harmless pieces. When an infection starts, these white blood cells respond immediately. The third line of defense takes a little longer to get started. This is provided by chemicals called antibodies that circulate through the bloodstream.

Antibodies are produced by smaller white blood cells called lymphocytes (LIM-fuh-syts). Invading organisms contain substances called antigens (ANT-i-juhnz) on their surfaces. The immune system uses the antigens to differentiate between these invaders and the body's own cells, and it produces antibodies that match them.

The structure of an antibody is specifically designed for each antigen. The two molecules fit together like a key in

These health workers are vaccinating a child in Somalia.

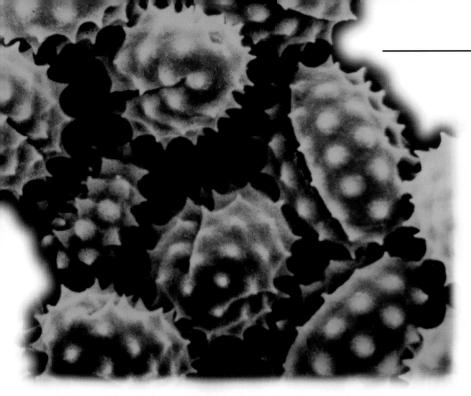

Grains of ragwort pollen seen through a scanning electron microscope. Some people suffer from hay fever in spring and summer due to an allergy to pollen.

a lock. Once an antibody has attached itself to an antigen, it acts as a signal to any nearby phagocytes to destroy the invader.

The antibody factory

The production of antibodies is controlled by a type of lymphocyte called a helper T-cell. These cells check for foreign objects in the blood. Once the helper T-cells identify an invader, they cause the local area to swell with more fluid, bringing in more phagocytes to deal with the pathogen. Some helper T-cells travel to the lymph nodes. The lymph nodes are glands dotted around the body. They contain lymphocytes called B-cells. The antigen pattern of the invader is transferred from the helper T-cell to the B-cell. The B-cell then multiplies into hundreds of copies of itself and begins to produce antibodies designed to attack the pathogen. Usually, one antibody will work well enough to deal with the invader.

Once the infection is over, a few of these helper T-cells and B-cells remain active in case the same pathogen returns. If it does, the immune system can deal with it much more quickly than during the first infection. This is called immunity.

Vaccines

Doctors have learned to work with the immune system to fight diseases. If a person has already been infected with a disease, doctors may give them a medicine called an antitoxin, which contains ready-made antibodies. People can also be given immunity to diseases before they have been exposed to them. This is done with medicines called vaccines. There are vaccines for many diseases, such as influenza and polio. Most are injected into the blood or into muscle, and some are eaten.

A vaccine contains the antigens of the pathogen. When these antigens are added to a person's blood, the immune system makes antibodies against the pathogen. The antigens in the vaccine are in a form that does not make the recipient develop the disease. Some vaccines contain antigens that have been extracted from the pathogen. Others contain pathogens that have been killed by heat but still contain antigens. Sometimes, vaccines containing live microorganisms are used—these may be a weakened version of the original pathogen, or from a closely related species.

The enemy within

The immune system can sometimes cause problems. Autoimmune diseases occur when the immune system begins to attack the body itself. Sometimes, these diseases attack the body as

HIGHLIGHTS

♦ Phagocytes are white blood cells that engulf and destroy pathogens.

♦ Antibodies attach themselves to pathogens and acts as a signal to other white blood cells.

♦ Vaccines use the immune system to produce immunity to many deadly diseases.

a whole. Other autoimmune diseases just affect one type of tissue. A very common autoimmune disease is rheumatoid arthritis (ROO-muh-toid ahr-THRI-tuhs). This disease inflames the joints of people of all ages.

The immune system can be a problem after an organ transplant. The system may recognize the new organ as a foreign body and begin to attack it. Some blood diseases are treated by bone marrow transplants. These are risky operations, because the transplanted bone marrow produces a new immune system that may regard the whole body as a foreign body.

Allergies are caused by the response of the immune system to harmless substances. These substances are called allergens. Common allergens are pollen, dust, and foods, such as peanuts and shellfish. When an allergen enters the body, the immune system produces a chemical called histamine (HIS-tuh-meen). Histamine causes blood vessels to leak fluid. Breathed-in allergens cause runny noses, sneezing, and itchy eyes. Other allergic reactions include rashes, sickness, and breathlessness. Extreme allergic reactions can cause breathing to cease and the heart to stop.

HIV and AIDS

The human immunodeficiency virus (HIV) infects T-cells, gradually wiping them out. This eventually leads to AIDS—acquired immune deficiency syndrome—where the immune system can no longer fight off attacks from pathogens. AIDS sufferers die from common, and normally nonlife-threatening diseases, such as pneumonia. More than 65 million people have been infected by the HIV virus, and at least 21 to 25 million people have died AIDS-related illnesses.

The HIV virus dupes the immune system by mutating constantly—each mutation causes a subtle change to the surface of the HIV virus so the immune system is unable to recognize it as an intruder. Powerful drugs have been developed that can delay the onset of AIDS. However, many sufferers live in poor regions and cannot afford these drugs.

CHECK THESE OUT!

✔ANTIBIOTICS ✔MEDICAL TECHNOLOGY

PEOPLE

Edward Jenner

Edward Jenner (1749–1823) was an English country doctor. Like many doctors in the 18th century, Jenner spent a lot of time treating people for smallpox, a deadly disease common at the time. He heard that people in Turkey injected themselves with a serum (fluid) made from the contents of smallpox sores. Some of these people suffered a minor bout of smallpox and were then immune. Others received a serious case of the disease and died because of it.

Jenner noticed that many of the local dairy farmers did not catch smallpox. They had suffered from cowpox, though. Cowpox is a similar but less deadly disease, caught from cattle. In 1796, Jenner decided to use a serum from cowpox sores as a vaccine against smallpox. He gave the serum to several of his patients, and each developed cowpox. Six weeks later, Jenner injected the same patients with smallpox serum. None of them developed the deadlier disease. After a massive program of vaccination, smallpox was finally wiped out by 1980.

Edward Jenner vaccinates 8-year-old James Phipps in 1796. Pus from the hand of Sarah Nelmes, a dairy maid, was used.

Information Theory

How information is sent and received

The amount of information sent around the world has increased enormously over the last 100 years. Messages are sent in many ways, by television and radio, computers and cellphones. In 1948, U.S. engineer Claude Elwood Shannon (born 1916) realized that no one really understood how to organize all the signals that were being produced. He proposed a theory that treated information as if it were a physical thing.

Codes

Reading a barcode with a scanner.

Shannon showed that information is only useful when it is sent and received. Before it can be sent, the information must be turned into a code that is suitable for the method of transmission. For example, messages sent by telephone wire need to be coded as electrical signals, while information sent along optical fibers take the form of pulses of light. Once the coded message has been received, it is decoded and translated back into its original form.

All information can be transformed into a binary code, which is made up of 1s and 0s. The smallest unit of information is one bit, which is short for "binary digit." A bit can be only 1 or 0.

HIGHLIGHTS

♦ Information theory treats information as a physical thing that can be measured.

♦ The smallest unit of information is a bit.

♦ Information must be turned into a code before it can be transmitted.

HOW DOES A BAR CODE WORK?

0   1 2 3 4 5   6 7 8 9 0   5

Bar codes contain two sets of data. The vertical black lines form a binary code, which is translated by a central computer to produce information on the price. The numbers refer to the manufacturer and product numbers.

Sending information

Information could be transmitted more efficiently by removing unnecessary information. For example, taking the vowels from words in a message will make it shorter but it will remain intelligible. Information can be compressed during coding. Imagine 100 flags, colored red, blue, and white. Fifty flags are red, 40 are blue, and 10 are white. This information could be sent as a binary message where 00 means red, 01 means blue, and 11 means white. The message will contain 200 bits—two for each flag.

However, this can be compressed by using fewer bits for the most common color and more for the least common color. Red can be represented as 0, blue as 10, and white as 110. This message only has 160 bits—1.6 per flag.

During transmission, a message can pick up errors. These errors are called noise. Noise might cause a 1 to be received as a 0, making the information incorrect.

CHECK THESE OUT!
✔CODES AND CIPHERS ✔COMPUTER

Insulation

Material that resists the transfer of heat, sound, or electricity

Insulation helps keep things warm, cool, or quiet. It also makes electrical equipment safe to use. Thermal insulation blocks heat, while acoustic (uh-KOO-stik) insulation blocks sound. Electrical insulation keeps electric currents safely inside power cords and cables.

Thermal insulation

Thermal insulation slows down the flow of heat from a warm area to a cooler one. Some materials, such as metals, let heat flow through them easily. This form of heat transfer is called conduction. Metal cooking pots conduct heat quickly from the stove to the food inside them. Other materials including plastic, wood, cork, and paper conduct heat poorly. These materials are known as thermal insulators. Cooking pots usually have handles of plastic or wood, which stay cool because they are thermal insulators.

Home insulation prevents heat escaping by conduction through the walls and roof. This helps keep the house warm in winter and cool in summer. Home insulation materials include fiberglass, rock wool, cork, and foamed plastic.

As well as traveling by conduction, heat can travel by radiation. This is the transfer of heat in the form of invisible waves. This radiation is also

called radiant heat. Dull black objects absorb and give out radiant heat. Aluminum foil is a good barrier to radiant heat. It reflects as much as 95 percent of the radiant heat falling on its surface.

A thermos bottle insulates hot or cold liquids by preventing heat from traveling in or out. The inner liner of the bottle has a double glass wall. The space between the two glass walls has almost all of the air pumped out. This reduces heat conduction between the two glass walls.

Acoustic insulation

Acoustic insulation (soundproofing) prevents the spread of unwanted noise. Some soundproofing absorbs sound and reduces the noise in a room. A lining of materials such as fiberglass and plastic foam absorbs sound inside a room or building. Heavy walls reflect sound and stop outside external sounds from entering a room.

Electrical insulation

In electrical cables, the wires that carry current are covered in insulating material that does not conduct electricity. This material is usually plastic. It stops short circuits caused by electricity jumping from one wire to another and protects people from electric shocks.

The floor of this new home under construction is being insulated with fiberglass batt held between wooden panels.

CHECK THESE OUT!
✔BUILDING TECHNIQUES
✔ELECTRICITY ✔METALS

Integrated Circuit

A complete electronic circuit in a single, miniature package

Electronics and the computer revolution of the 20th century were largely brought about by the integrated circuit, or silicon chip. Invented in the late 1950s, the integrated circuit squeezes thousands of tiny electronic components onto a single piece of silicon called a chip. Integrated circuits transformed computers from monsters the size of a room into modern palmtops. They made possible a range of other electronic devices, including cellular phones and pocket calculators.

Making connections

A device such as a television set contains many different circuits built from electronic components. Different components, such as resistors, capacitors, diodes, and transistors, are put together to make circuits that do different things. The more complex the job a circuit has to do, the more components are needed to do it. The more components there are in a circuit, the larger the circuit will be, and the more space it takes up. The larger the circuit is, the more power it will use, and the more likely it is to malfunction (go wrong).

In the late 1950s, two U.S. scientists figured out a better way to build complicated electronic circuits. Instead of connecting many separate components together, they made microscopic patterns and connections on the surface of a piece of silicon. These patterns and connections were called integrated circuits, because many different components were brought together, or integrated, into a small space.

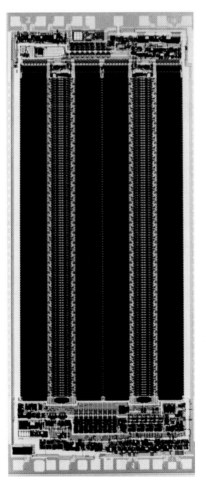

HIGHLIGHTS

◆ Integrated circuits consist of electronic components and the connections between them on the surface of a semiconductor such as silicon.

◆ Integrated circuits are also known as silicon chips.

◆ Cellular phones and modern computers of all sizes rely on silicon chips.

Making integrated circuits

Most materials can be divided into two types—those that conduct electricity (conductors) and those that do not (insulators). Semiconductor materials, like silicon and germanium, fall between these extremes. They have a small conductivity in their pure forms, which can become large when the right impurities are added. If silicon is treated (or doped) with other elements, it can be made to conduct electricity in one of two ways. If silicon is doped with arsenic or phosphorus, it carries an electric current by allowing tiny subatomic particles called electrons to move in one direction. This is known as a negative-type or n-type semiconductor. If doped with boron or antimony, it carries a current by allowing electrons to move in the other direction. This is known as a positive-type or p-type semiconductor.

Electronic components such as diodes, capacitors, and transistors can be made by placing n-type and p-type silicon next to one

A greatly enlarged view of a silicon chip, an integrated circuit.

An industrial robot places a tray of silicon wafers into an acid bath.

another in different patterns. Producing a complete integrated circuit involves figuring out how to arrange the different areas of n-type and p-type silicon to make components. A pattern of connections between components has to be designed with great care. The circuit is manufactured by placing the components and the connections on the surface of a silicon wafer.

The whole process of making an integrated circuit is very precise. The circuits are made in a room where the air is constantly filtered. A room such as this is called a "clean room." Workers wear protective coats and hats to prevent them from introducing dirt.

The starting point for an integrated circuit is a large crystal of silicon that has been grown in the shape of a cylinder. The surface is polished, then sliced into thin circular wafers. Dozens of tiny silicon chips are made side-by-side on each wafer.

PEOPLE

Jack Kilby and Robert Noyce

In 1952, English scientist Geoffrey Dummer (born 1909) had the idea of a microchip. His prototype failed. A few years later, two U.S. electrical engineers invented the integrated circuit independently and at almost exactly the same time. In 1958, Jack Kilby (born 1923), of Texas Instruments, created a circuit of resistors, capacitors, and transistors on a tiny wafer of silicon. He connected them with gold wires. In 1959, Robert Noyce (1927–1990), of Fairchild Semiconductor, figured out how to build the connections into a circuit by making them part of the pattern on a silicon chip. After a long court battle, Texas Instruments and Fairchild Semiconductor agreed to share the invention.

Components are made first by creating areas of p-type and n-type silicon. This is done by firing electrically charged atoms, called ions, of a gas at the silicon wafer. This process is called sputtering. Areas of p-type and n-type silicon can also be created by allowing a vapor to condense on the surface of the wafer. This process is called vapor deposition.

The connections between the p-type and n-type areas are made in much the same way that artists paint patterns through the lines of a stencil. Chip makers use photographic "masks" rather than stencils. They use light and acid instead of paint to draw the pattern of electrical connections on the silicon wafer.

Types of integrated circuits

The two main types of circuits are analog, which transmit continuously varying electrical signals, and digital, which usually process numbers. Amplifiers are among the most common analog circuits. Amplifiers take an electronic signal and make it stronger. Microprocessors are the best-known digital circuits. Built into the heart of computers, pocket calculators, and cellular phones, microprocessors are entire computers on a single chip, sometimes containing thousands of separate electronic components.

CHECK THESE OUT!
✔COMPUTER ✔MICROMACHINE
✔NANOTECHNOLOGY

Intensive Care Unit

Part of a hospital where seriously ill patients are treated

Intensive care units (ICUs) are small hospital wards where very seriously ill patients can be given the attention they need. Patients in an ICU may have just had major surgery, suffered a heart attack, or been badly injured in an accident.

Each ICU bed is equipped with machines that monitor the patient's blood pressure, body temperature, breathing, and heartbeat. Some patients may have the level of oxygen in their blood checked. Patients with head injuries will have the pressure of the liquids inside the brain measured. All this information is displayed on screens at a central area. ICU staff can check the health of all the patients in the ward on these screens at the same time.

Inside an ICU

Many ICU patients need a ventilator, a machine that pumps air through the mouth of a patient who cannot breathe independently. Air is pushed

out again by the elasticity of the lungs and ribs. If a patient needs a ventilator for a long time, a tube is stuck into the throat through a hole made in the neck. Air from the ventilator passes through a humidifier that adds moisture. This stops the patient's lungs from drying out. Patients on a ventilator cannot eat by themselves. Instead, they must receive fluids and medicine through a tube attached to a blood vessel in the arm.

Each patient in an ICU takes up twice as much space as a patient in a regular ward. A typical ICU will have between four and 12 beds. Large hospitals may have more than one ICU. Modern hospitals need space for one ICU patient for every 100 nonurgent patients.

An ICU has only one entrance to prevent people from walking through on the way to somewhere else. There needs to be a laboratory nearby, so tests can be done quickly. Many ICUs are equipped with portable X-ray machines so patients do not need to be moved unnecessarily. The emergency room and operating room are also nearby. Many larger hospitals have ICUs designed for particular problems. Serious burns are treated in specialized ICUs. Babies that have been born too early go to their own ICU. These wards contain monitoring equipment designed for these tiny patients.

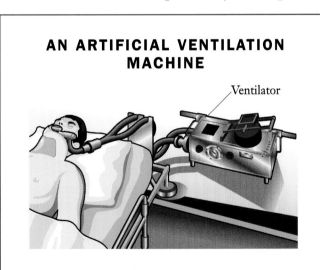

AN ARTIFICIAL VENTILATION MACHINE

Ventilator

When a person can no longer breathe naturally, artificial ventilation may be used instead. In this process, air is transmitted to the patient's lungs through a tube inserted in the windpipe. After the lungs are filled, the air is expelled by the natural elasticity of the lungs.

CHECK THESE OUT!
✔MEDICAL IMAGING ✔MEDICAL TECHNOLOGY

Internet

A worldwide network of linked computers that can share information

The rapid growth of personal computing and improvements in computer technology have both contributed to the growth of the Internet. This resource can be described as an electronic library of books, data, film, pictures, and music. Internet users can find answers to questions, send and receive electronic messages and computer documents instantly, shop in another country, sample new music, download the latest software, play games, make new friends, or just surf for fun.

The structure of the Internet

The Internet consists of a series of national and global wide-area networks, or WANs. All the computers in a WAN are linked through powerful computers called routers. Routers select the best ways to pass information from one place to the next. They base this selection on where the information is being sent and how busy a network is. This ensures that information passes along a network as quickly as possible. In areas where the Internet is used a lot, a regional hub gathers information from all the computers

HIGHLIGHTS

◆ The Internet is a series of computer networks linked worldwide by routers.

◆ Computers use a set of rules called TCP/IP to send information in small packets by the fastest available routes.

◆ The Internet has many applications, including e-mail and the World Wide Web.

within a region. The hub then sends this information, in bulk, to the closest router. Other important parts of the Internet include satellite bands and fiber optic cables. These technologies provide links between routers and from the routers to users of the Internet or clients. The client may be the owner of a home PC or a large server computer in an office building. The server distributes information to each computer in the office.

An Internet identity

Accessing the Internet is simple. A client needs a computer, a modem, an Internet Protocol (IP) number, and a domain name. Every computer accessing the Internet has its own IP number, which looks something like this: 149.174.211.5. The domain name corresponds to the IP number but it is much easier to remember. For example, the domain name "someone@somewhere.com" could correspond to the IP number 149.174.211.5.

Most clients hold an account with an Internet Service Provider (ISP). ISPs are corporations that allow clients to access the Internet using ISP servers so that the clients do not have to operate a server themselves.

With the growth of the World Wide Web, people began to use Internet cafes to find information or to read and send e-mail.

Packets of information

Information passes through a computer network in a series of small packets. Information is broken down into packets and sent according to a set of rules called TCP/IP (Transmission Control Protocol/Internet Protocol). A similar process reassembles the data on arrival. This is called packet switching. Routers direct the packets along the fastest route through the network. All computers send and receive information using TCP/IP.

Modems, ISDN, cable, and DSL

Computers are digital machines. They read information as a sequence of zeros and ones. While links between telephone exchanges are now digital, individual telephone lines are not. These lines are not suitable for digital communication, so computers must convert the signals they carry into digital signals. The conversion requires a set of rules, or protocol,

The latest generation of mobile phones allows users to access the World Wide Web without a landline connection.

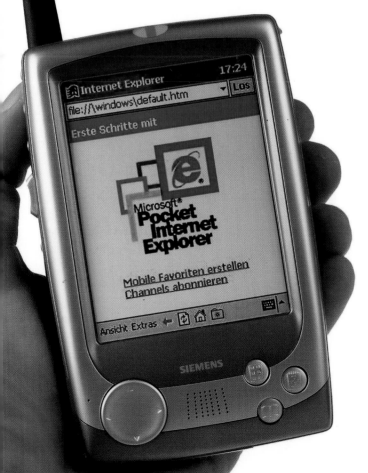

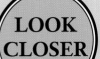

LOOK CLOSER

Nets

The Internet is the global network of tens of thousands of computer networks, which are interconnected and accessible to the public. However, when only two or more computer networks are linked the resulting network is called an internet. These internets can be local, inter-state, or inter-company, for example. The private computer network of a company, government body, or academic institution is called an intranet. The computer software used by machines linked on an intranet is the same as that used on the Internet, but an intranet can only be accessed internally within a company or an institution. An extranet is an intranet network, parts of which can be accessed, for example by the public or other companies to place orders for products.

and a modem or ISDN card. The cheapest and most popular way to connect to the Internet is by using a modem. The modem takes the digital sequence of 0s and 1s from the computer and converts them into the type of signal a telephone line can carry, an analog signal. The modem also converts incoming analog signals into digital signals. External modems plug into the back of a computer's hard drive. Internal modems fit into a slot, called a bus, inside the computer's hard drive. Most modems operate at 56 kilobytes per second—this means the modem can transmit around 56,000 characters (such as a letter or a number) every second.

An ISDN (Integrated Services Digital Network) link is another way of connecting to the Internet. ISDN converts the analog link between the client's telephone and the digital telephone exchange into a digital system. This increases the capacity for sending information and speeds up the connection. However, the line connection and call charges are more expensive.

Modern developments called cable access and DSL ensure faster and cheaper connection to the Internet. Because cable Internet access uses the same lines as cable television, it is only available in certain areas. Cable access works at around 10 megabytes per second (180 times faster than a modem), but clients have to share communication space with other clients. The more people connecting to the Internet through the cable, the slower the Internet access. DSL (Digital Subscriber Line) is the fastest option of all. DSL works at speeds of up to 6 megabytes per second using a normal telephone system. Both DSL and cable access are widespread across much of North America.

The wonders of the Web

The World Wide Web allows clients to access information from all over the world. The Web uses hypertext, a system that displays text and images on the screen of a computer in the form of a Web page. Individual words or pictures on each Web page may act as electronic links (hyperlinks) to other Web pages or information such as a picture or video clip.

English computer scientist Tim Berners-Lee (born 1955) developed the World Wide Web in 1990. He wrote the original Hypertext Mark-up Language (HTML), the language that computers use to display Web pages. A computer reads Web pages using a set of rules called HyperText

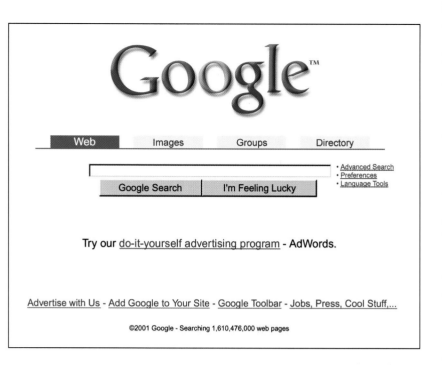

*Search engines, such as **Google**, trawl through millions of web pages to match a word or phrase.*

Transfer Protocol (HTTP). Each Web page is given an address called a Uniform Resource Locator (URL). The URL is a series of characters that spells out the location of the Web page on the Web. All URLs have a so-called domain type. Common examples are ".com" for a company or commercial organization or ".gov" for a government body. Many URLs also contain a country code, such as ".uk" for the United Kingdom and ".de" for Germany.

Search engines

The main problem with the Web is its size. To find particular information among millions of Web pages, a search engine is needed. After entering a simple keyword or phrase into a text box, the search engine searches for and displays hyperlinks to all the Web sites and pages that contain that word or phrase.

Most search engines present information in organized categories. There are even search agents that perform searches using more than one search engine at the same time.

CHECK THESE OUT!
✔COMPUTER ✔DIGITAL TECHNOLOGY
✔TELEPHONY AND TELEGRAPHY

LOOK CLOSER

E-mail

Electronic mail, or e-mail, is the one of the most popular uses of the Internet. Using e-mail, clients send messages from one computer to another almost instantly. Each client has an e-mail address in the form of "username@domainname.com." Using a set of rules called Simple Mail Transfer Protocol (SMTP), e-mail is sent over the Internet to the server with the correct domain name.

The e-mail is stored there until the person it is addressed to logs on. When that happens, the waiting message downloads onto that person's computer. Clients can also send pictures, documents, music, and even whole computer programs in the form of attachments. Every Internet Service Provider provides e-mail to its clients.

Inventions

Creating new tools, processes, or products

Inventions are different from discoveries. A discovery is something that already exists but is recognized or understood for the first time. The process of invention involves people manufacturing something, or using something natural in a new way. Some inventions are machines, such as can openers, dishwashers, and vacuum cleaners. Other are new processes, such as papermaking.

Most inventions come about because of the need for a particular tool, or a way to solve a problem. Some inventions that at first seemed useless, even to their creators, later turned about to be very important. Still others have come accidentally as by-products of research into completely different areas.

Most modern inventions are made by scientists or engineers that are employed to solve technical problems. Large companies employ teams of their own research and development (R&D) scientists, or pay for research in universities. Sometimes, scientists are paid to do pure research that has no immediate use, partly because it is difficult to predict which inventions will be useful in the future. For example, just a few decades ago, few people would have predicted the present importance of information technology, including the Internet and e-mail.

These are clockwork radios.
English inventor Trevor Baylis (born 1937) was concerned by the lack of effective communication over large areas of the developing world, where many people do not have access to electricity to operate radios. The clockwork radio proved a cheap, reliable, and environmentally friendly solution.

The ability to invent

Since ancient times, inventions have allowed people to alter their surroundings to make life easier. The ability to invent tools and shape the natural world is, according to many people, a unique human quality.

Making even a simple tool requires the ability to think in terms of things that cannot be seen immediately. This type of thinking is called abstract thought. The toolmaker must be able to recognize a problem and search for a solution and must decide which raw material is best for a job. The toolmaker must also imagine how the raw material can be changed to suit its new purpose. The ability to invent has allowed people to invent hundreds of thousands of new processes and tools over the course of human history.

HIGHLIGHTS

◆ Invention is the process of creating a new tool, process, or product.

◆ The driving forces behind invention through the ages have included religion, profit, and the military.

◆ Many inventions have been developed as by-products of research in other fields; the space race led to many inventions used in the home.

Reasons to invent

Humans first started making tools more than two million years ago. The oldest inventions discovered by archeologists to date are shaped flint tools that were used to hunt and dismember (cut up) wild animals. Throughout human history, inventions have been driven by various forces, from survival to the desire to increase productivity and make a profit.

Religion was once a major force driving invention. During the first century C.E., the Greek inventor Hero of Alexandria created "magic" temple doors that opened automatically. They were driven by a burst of hot air that was produced when a high priest lit a fire on the altar. The first calendars and clocks were also invented for religious purposes.

A patron is someone who supports or employs a person such as an inventor to produce new devices. In the past, wealthy patrons made many inventions possible. For example, various Chinese emperors patronized the scientists who devised gunpowder, printing, and other inventions, centuries before their use was adopted by western countries. Later in Europe, wealthy landowners commissioned scientists to develop new types of mills and other inventions. Patronage by industry continued to support inventors until the mid-19th century.

In 1885, German Gottlieb Daimler (1834–1900) developed a carriage powered by an internal combustion engine.

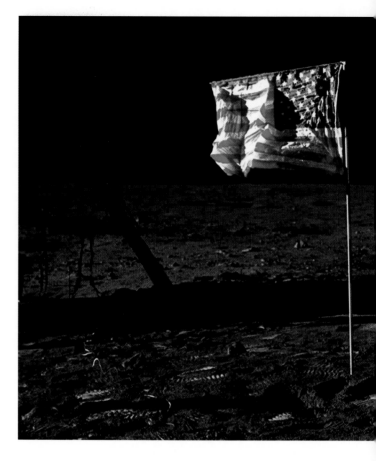

The need for battlefield superiority has also driven invention. From ancient times, cities and states poured huge resources into developing new weapons and ways to defend themselves. During the mid-20th century, rivalry rather than outright war between the Soviet Union and the United States led to the Sputnik missions and the Apollo Moon landings. Enormous sums were invested in developing these space programs. Inventions such as nonstick frying pans and microchips were spin-offs from the space race.

Even before money was invented, new devices from the plow to the potter's wheel helped ancient societies increase productivity. Most modern inventions are tightly linked to profit and sales. Businesses are interested in new products and processes that will give them an edge over their rivals. Products that go on sale to the public must not only work well, but they must also be easy to use and pleasing to look at.

The U.S. Apollo landings represent a pinnacle of invention. Here, astronaut Buzz Aldrin (born 1930) walks on the lunar surface.

How inventions come about

The breakthrough that leads to an invention often occurs because people are dissatisfied with the current state of affairs. Improvements are often made by scientists or engineers that know of the difficulties present in a particular area. Inspiration rarely strikes out of the blue, but as a result of hard thinking about a problem.

Lateral thinking is often important for inventors. This is a talent for looking at one thing, such as a flint, and seeing it in a new context—as a tool, for example. In the past, great inventors such as Leonardo da Vinci (1452–1519) were knowledgeable in many fields, such as science, mathematics, music, and the arts, allowing them to see how a solution from one area might help overcome a problem in another.

Most new inventions result from the application of scientific knowledge. The Greeks were the first to develop scientific methods, based on theory, experiment, and careful observation. In turn, the Romans put Greek ideas to many practical purposes and devised many new inventions.

The timing of inventions

Luck and coincidence often seem to play a part in invention. There are many stories of inventions that occurred after a stroke of luck allowed a vital breakthrough to take place. In some cases, however, it is likely that someone else would soon have made the breakthrough if the breakthrough had not occurred when it did.

The invention of the automobile is a good example of this. German engineers Gottlieb Daimler (1834–1900) and Karl Benz (1844–1929) are credited with the invention of the automobile in 1885. However, several inventors from other countries were working on similar ideas at the same time. The invention of the automobile was boosted by the development of the internal combustion engine, which in turn was influenced by the discovery of oil reserves and the new science of organic chemistry. In this way, every useful invention is the product of a chain of earlier inventions, going all the way back to flint tools, the wheel, and harnessing fire.

CHECK THESE OUT:
✔AUTOMOBILE ✔FLIGHT ✔SPACE TRAVEL ✔WHEEL

PEOPLE

Leonardo da Vinci

Leonardo da Vinci (1452–1519) was a great artist, a talented scientist, and a prolific inventor. During his career, Leonardo spent time working as a military engineer for the state of Milan, in Italy. Throughout his adult life, he kept a series of notebooks that record his many new practical ideas.

Leonardo was way ahead of his time. He grasped the principles of machines such as helicopters and armored tanks, which could not have been built during his lifetime. Many of his inventions were immediately useful, however, such as the ball bearing. He also invented the parachute and the first clock with a minute hand.

Iron and Steel

Strong materials obtained from iron ore

Iron is the most important metal used by people. It is essential for modern industry, agriculture, and transportation. Many objects, from paper clips to bridges, are made of steel. Steel is iron that has been treated to make it stronger. Many everyday items made from wood, glass, plastic, and other materials are produced using steel tools and steel machines.

Iron ore

Deep below the surface, Earth is made from mainly liquid iron. In the thin, rocky crust of the planet's surface, iron is also a very common metal. Only aluminum is more abundant. Iron naturally occurs as iron ore. Ore is rock that contains a lot of metal. There are several types of iron ore. Most are rocks that contain a lot of iron oxide. Iron oxide is a rust-like chemical produced when iron combines with oxygen gas in the air. The most common iron ores are hematite (hee-muh-TYT) and magnetite (mag-nuh-TYT). Hematite is red and contains slightly less iron than magnetite, which is black.

Making iron

Iron was first removed from ore about 2000 B.C.E. by a people called the Hittites who lived in what is now Turkey.

HIGHLIGHTS

- Iron is removed from its ore by heating it with charcoal or coke in a furnace.

- Steel is a type of iron that has a little carbon mixed in with it, to make it tougher.

- In modern steel production, liquid iron is blasted with oxygen gas to remove impurities.

At this time, people could already extract (remove) copper metal from its ore. At first, charcoal was used to extract metal from oxide. Charcoal is made of mainly carbon. When it is burned along with an oxide ore, the carbon gradually takes the oxygen away from the ore. The result of this process, called reduction, is carbon dioxide gas and pure metal.

When the reduction process is done with iron, however, some of the charcoal mixes with the metal and makes a solid substance. This substance is very hard but it shatters easily. The iron has to be purified by a further process, in which the iron is heated until it becomes soft. Then, it is hit repeatedly with a hammer. This action breaks up the charcoal and the ash mixed in with metal, squeezing them out. The result is a very pure form of iron, known as wrought iron.

Skyscrapers, such as these in New York City, could not be constructed without the use of a steel frame that takes the weight of the building to the ground. The tallest skyscrapers are built from several steel frames.

Ancient peoples used two types of furnaces. A bowl furnace was little more than a hole in the ground. The furnace was kept hot by using bellows to pump air into it through a pipe. The other type of furnace was called a shaft furnace, which was stone-built. Shaft furnaces relied on rising heat to draw air into the burning mixture of ore and charcoal. These early furnaces could not be made any hotter than 2100°F (1150°C). At this temperature, iron is still a solid, known as bloom. After the bloom was turned into wrought iron, the metal was shaped into useful objects.

About 4,000 years ago, iron began to replace copper as the most important metal. Iron was more valuable than copper because it was tougher and more flexible. In addition, two pieces of iron could be joined together by heating them to a high temperature and hammering them. This was an early form of welding. Unlike copper objects, iron tools and weapons could be repaired if they broke.

Advances in iron production

Ironworkers experimented with different amounts of ore and charcoal. Iron produced using a lot of charcoal has more carbon in it. Metal like this is called cast iron. Because of the larger amount of carbon in cast iron, it melts at a lower temperature. However, it also makes the metal very brittle. This type of iron makes simple, solid shapes when poured into molds.

Cast iron was first widely used in China. By the Middle Ages, northern Europeans used waterwheels to power mechanical bellows. These more powerful bellows could increase the temperature of a furnace to around 2200°F (1200°C). Hotter furnaces produced liquid iron that had a lot of carbon in it. This metal was cast into objects such as cannons.

By the 15th century, iron was produced by furnaces that resembled modern blast furnaces. A blast furnace is a shaft furnace that has an air supply forced through it. In early blast furnaces, the liquid metal flowed through a central channel into several molds, where it cooled into a solid. The arrangement of the furnace and the molds reminded people of a sow suckling its piglets. Because of this resemblance, iron that is made in blast furnaces is still called pig iron. The

liquid pig iron was refined into wrought iron by having air bubbling through it. This process burned away the carbon.

Early steel

Steel contains a little more carbon than wrought iron, but much less than cast iron. The carbon in cast iron is in large chunks that weaken the iron. This makes the metal brittle. However, the carbon in steel is thoroughly mixed with the iron, which strengthens the metal. This is why steel is tougher than pure wrought iron.

Nearly 3,000 years ago, the Egyptians made steel into steel knives and swords. The Chinese used steel from 206 B.C.E. Knowledge of steel did not reach Japan until about 1000 C.E., when it was used to make samurai swords.

Steel production was the main driving force behind the Industrial Revolution, which swept across Britain and then the world in the 18th century. The Industrial Revolution was a time of great change in industry when steampower-driven machinery was introduced. In 1709, Abraham Darby (1678–1717), an English

PEOPLE

Henry Bessemer

Henry Bessemer (1813–1898) was an English engineer and inventor who had developed a type of gun that required a very strong cast iron. As he investigated how to make the strong metal, he figured out how to produce steel on a large scale. Bessemer noticed that blowing air through cast iron made the iron stronger and heated up the liquid metal so it could be poured more easily. The blast of air burned out some of the carbon, combining with it to make carbon monoxide gas and releasing heat. Bessemer built a vessel known as a converter. His converter was designed for each stage of the steel-making process: charging with molten iron, blowing with air, and then tipping out the steel. U.S. inventor, William Kelly (1811–1888) developed an identical process the same year as Bessemer. However, Bessemer's name was given to the converter. Converters, similar to the one designed by Bessemer, are used still in modern steelworks.

ironmaster, began using coke instead of charcoal in iron production. Coke is a treated form of coal that has had many of its impurities removed. Since coke is harder than charcoal, it does not collapse as easily as it burns. When charcoal collapses, it can cause the fire to go out. After coke was introduced, more ore and more coke could be packed into a blast furnace at a time. Darby's furnace soon produced up to 10 tons (9 metric tons) of pig iron a week. Darby also used steam-driven bellows to create a stronger jet of air inside the furnace.

In 1784, English ironmaster Henry Cort (1740–1800) developed the puddling process to convert pig iron into wrought iron. He melted pig iron with some iron ore in a furnace to form a puddle of metal. He then stirred the puddle. During stirring, the oxygen in the iron ore combined with carbon mixed with the pig iron to produce carbon monoxide gas. This gas bubbled out of the puddle of iron. Other impurities in the pig iron formed a liquid called slag, which floated on top of the thick puddle of iron. The slag was scraped off the top of the metal, which was then left to cool into wrought iron.

Steel production

In the 1850s, English engineer Henry Bessemer (1813–1898) developed a process to convert pig iron into steel. The process involved blowing air into the liquid iron. As in the puddling process, carbon combines with oxygen, and the slag floats on top of the iron. Bessemer's process is better than puddling because it can be done on a much larger scale. The burning carbon also keeps the mixture warm. However, there are problems using blown air. In this process, nitrogen gas becomes mixed with the metal, making it weaker. Another problem is how to control the amount of carbon left in the finished steel. English scientist Robert Mushet (1811–1891) discovered that adding an alloy (mixture of metals) made from iron, manganese, and carbon adjusted the level of carbon in the finished steel.

Soon after Bessemer introduced his process, another way to make steel was developed. German-born British industrialist William Siemens (1823–1883) and his brother Friedrich (1826–1904) invented the regenerative oven. This oven had a broad, shallow stream of burning fuel. Air flowed through the oven and was blasted down into it from above. The mixture of fuel and air was heated up in a stack of bricks near the entrance to the oven. Hot gases from the oven were collected in an identical stack of bricks at the other end of the oven. The direction of this stream of fuel was reversed every now and then to make the most of this extra heat.

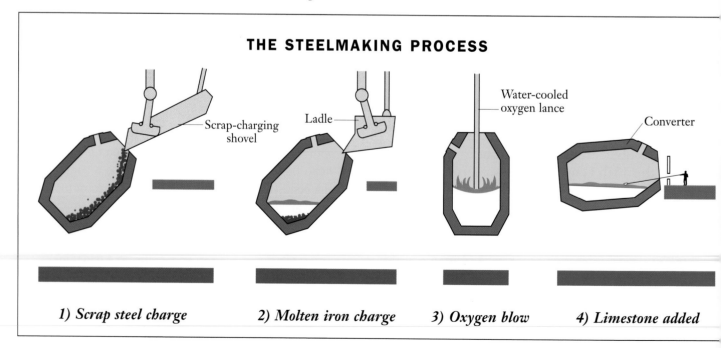

THE STEELMAKING PROCESS

Scrap-charging shovel

Ladle

Water-cooled oxygen lance

Converter

1) Scrap steel charge   *2) Molten iron charge*   *3) Oxygen blow*   *4) Limestone added*

French steelmaker Pierre-Émile Martin (1824–1915) used the regenerative oven to make steel that was better than the metal produced by Bessemer converters. Martin's method became known as the open-hearth process. Until the middle of the 20th century, most of the world's steel was made by the open-hearth method. Around a sixth of all steel is still made in this way.

Modern steelmaking

Bessemer realized that his process would have been much more effective if it used pure oxygen, instead of air. Before the 20th century, however, pure oxygen was not easy to make. In the 1940s, pure oxygen, extracted by cooling the gases in air into liquids, was used for the first time in steel production in two purpose-built steel plants in Austria. Each one could produce 35 tons (32 metric tons) of steel in a single run. Most modern steelworks are set up in a similar way to these two plants.

Blast furnaces and steel converters are located on the same site. A modern blast furnace operates continuously and can produce 10,000

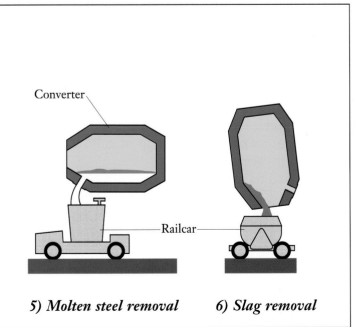

5) *Molten steel removal*   6) *Slag removal*

Molten iron from a blast furnace is poured from a ladle into a Bessemer converter to make steel.

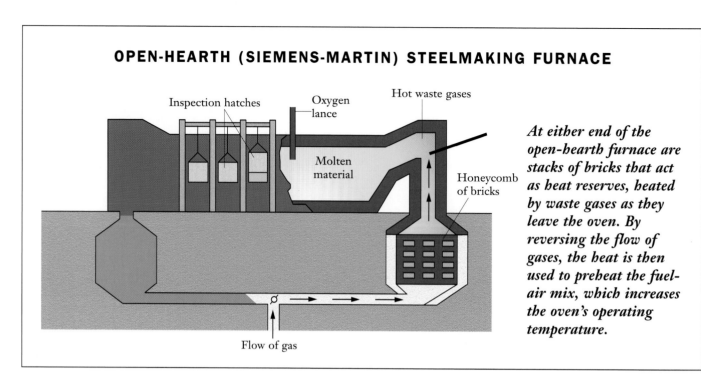

OPEN-HEARTH (SIEMENS-MARTIN) STEELMAKING FURNACE

Inspection hatches

Oxygen lance

Hot waste gases

Molten material

Honeycomb of bricks

Flow of gas

At either end of the open-hearth furnace are stacks of bricks that act as heat reserves, heated by waste gases as they leave the oven. By reversing the flow of gases, the heat is then used to preheat the fuel-air mix, which increases the oven's operating temperature.

tons (9,070 metric tons) of liquid iron every day. As well as carbon, the iron also contains silicon, sulfur, manganese, and phosphorus.

Hot metal is poured out of the furnace into huge ladles that can carry 350 tons (320 metric tons) each. As the ladle moves to the converter, the metal inside is treated to remove some of its impurities. The converter is similar to Bessemer's original design—a large cylinder, which is open at one end. It can be swung all the way around, even upside down. The converter is lined with heat-resistant bricks made of magnesium carbonate. The converters are loaded through the top. Before iron is poured in, scrap steel is added—this absorbs some of the heat during the conversion process and stops the temperature from getting too high. After the iron is added, a water-cooled lance is lowered into the converter.

Oxygen is blown through the lance into the metal at twice the speed of sound. Limestone is added at this stage to combine with impurities to form slag. The oxygen is blown into the converter for about 20 minutes. Toward the end of the process, sensors are lowered into the metal to check the temperature and the level of carbon present.

Any carbon monoxide gas produced during the blow is collected and used as a fuel elsewhere in the plant. After the oxygen is turned off, the converter is tilted onto its side, and liquid steel is poured out through a hole. Then, the converter is tilted upside down to empty out the slag. Plants using this method can produce 5 million tons (4.5 million metric tons) of steel a year.

Secondary steel making

It is often necessary to process the steel further after the conversion. This is known as secondary steel making, and it produces steel with different properties. Secondary steel making is generally carried out while the steel is still liquid. Metals that are to be mixed in with the steel are added as wire or ground-up powder. The steel may also be put into a vacuum, an area where all gases have been sucked out. This draws out gases, such as nitrogen, that might be mixed in with the steel. Once the steel has been processed, it is cast into a continuous strip of solid metal and cut into sections.

It is hard to control the temperature in a converter. This makes it difficult to control the exact contents of the steel being made. When it is important for steel to have exactly the right amount of carbon and other chemicals in it, steel makers use an electric arc furnace. In an arc furnace, the metal is melted by three giant electrodes (conductors of electricity) made from graphite. Limestone and oxygen are added to speed up the conversion. Using electricity to melt metal is more expensive than using a fuel, so furnaces like these are only used to make steel that requires exact amounts of carbon.

Types of steel

There are thousands of types of steel, made by adding certain chemicals or by heating and working the steel in different ways. There are two main types, however: carbon steel and alloy steels. Most of the world's steel is carbon steel, which can be low-, medium-, or high-carbon. Alloy steels contain a mixture of other metals.

Low-carbon steel is also called mild steel. It contains only 0.25 percent carbon and is easy to cut, bend, and weld into shapes. Low-carbon steel is used to make everything from cars and trucks to nails. It is strengthened by alloying with nickel, copper, and other metals. This metal is used to make pistons, machine parts, and other tough objects. Medium-carbon steel has up to 0.6 percent carbon. It is very hard-wearing but more brittle than mild steel. It is used in railroad car wheels and machine parts. High-carbon steel has up to 1.5 percent carbon. It is very hard and is used to make knives and razor blades.

Stainless steel is the most familiar alloy steel. It contains 11 percent chromium, a very shiny metal. Chromium reacts with oxygen in the air to create a film of oxide that coats the surface of the object. This film prevents the iron in the steel

PEOPLE

Andrew Carnegie

Andrew Carnegie (1835–1919) founded the modern steel industry in the United States. He was born in Scotland but moved with his family to Pennsylvania when he was 12. He began working in the railroad industry, but after several trips to Britain, Carnegie decided to set up a steelworks near Pittsburgh. This steelworks was the first in the United States to make use of the newly developed Bessemer converter. Carnegie became a very rich man by buying into all parts of the steel industry. He owned mines that produced iron ore and coal that could be turned into coke. He also owned the railroads and ships that transported these raw materials to the steelworks. After he retired, Carnegie gave away much of his fortune. The money was used to create institutions, such as the Carnegie Technical Institute, later to become the Carnegie-Mellon University, in Pittsburgh, and Carnegie Hall in New York City.

from rusting. Stainless steel is used to make surgical instruments, knives and forks, and other shiny objects. Manganese steel, sometimes called Hadfield steel, contains 12 percent manganese. This type of steel is very resistant to wear and is used in crushing equipment and piano wires.

CHECK THESE OUT!
✔BLAST FURNACE ✔CIVIL ENGINEERING
✔ENGINEERING ✔METALS

Steel is one of the standard materials used to construct bridges. This is the Commodore Barry bridge, which crosses the Delaware River.

Irrigation

The supply of water to farmland using canals, ditches, or pipes

Irrigation is a way of supplying water to land where the soil is too dry for crops to grow. Water is carried to fields by artificial channels. Irrigated land is often also drained to prevent soil from becoming waterlogged. Irrigation and drainage allow farmers to grow crops in many areas that would otherwise be barren.

In dry regions such as much of the Middle East, farming would be impossible without irrigation. In other places, irrigation is used to add to the natural water supplies provided by rainfall to increase crop yields.

History of irrigation

Irrigation is a very ancient practice. By 7000 B.C.E, farmers in Mesopotamia (modern Iraq) were irrigating the dry, flat plains that lay between the Tigris and Euphrates Rivers to create fertile cropland. Five thousand years ago, the Egyptians built raised banks, or levees, along the Nile River to regulate flooding of the adjoining farmland. In both these regions, irrigation techniques allowed farmers to bring more land under cultivation. Over the centuries, irrigation techniques have improved, and more land has been irrigated.

Experts estimate that a total area of around 600 million acres (242 million hectares) is currently irrigated worldwide. Much of this land is in Asia, where the main food crop, rice, is grown in flooded fields called paddies. The

In drier parts of the United States, sprinklers are used in yards to water grass and flowers.

countries with the largest areas of irrigated land are China, India, Pakistan, and the United States. In the United States about 50 million acres (20 million hectares) of land are under irrigation, mostly in the western states.

Traditional irrigation

Simple irrigation techniques developed centuries ago are still used in many parts of the world. Water is drawn from a source such as a lake or river. It is then carried to the fields using a network of ditches or pipes and is distributed to the crop. The land may be watered by flooding, or irrigated using shallow furrows.

This water is usually raised from the source to a higher level, from where it flows down a slope. A number of traditional water-lifting devices were used, such as the shaduf. Water is now raised using motor-driven pumps.

HIGHLIGHTS

- ◆ Irrigation is the supply of water to farmland, so crops can be grown on it.

- ◆ Irrigation water is drawn from a river, carried to the fields in ditches, pipes, or canals, and then distributed to the crop.

- ◆ Irrigation water is applied to fields on the surface, underground, or by sprinklers.

Modern irrigation methods

Modern irrigation methods work on the same principles as traditional ones but use the latest technology to raise, transport, and deliver water to fields. Irrigation systems are designed carefully before construction begins. Engineers analyze the soil in the area to find out how much water it can hold and whether it is permeable (allows water to pass through it). They also consider the climate, the amount of water needed for the crops that will be grown, and how irrigation will affect the local environment and wildlife. The first problem is to find a suitable water source with sufficient water of a reasonable quality. The source must continue to refill at least as fast as water is drawn from it, or it will dry up eventually. At the source, the water quality is checked to discover if it is polluted or very salty, or contains so much silt that it would quickly clog up the irrigation system.

Most irrigation water is drawn from a river, lake, or an underground water supply called an aquifer (AK-wuh-fuhr). Crops usually need the most water during hot, dry periods when sources have the least water, so a way to store water is required. Irrigation water is often stored in artificial lakes called reservoirs, many of which are created by building dams.

Once the source is established, engineers plan a way to transport the water to the fields. This is done using a network of canals, ditches, or pipes. In modern times, canals are often lined with concrete to prevent leaks and to deter plants from growing in the channel. Pipes may be made

A farmer adjusts a siphon in an irrigated field of lettuce in Arizona.

of concrete, ceramic, plastic, or metal. They are expensive to lay but reduce the amount of water lost through evaporation. Some modern irrigation systems are equipped with valves or regulators that control the amount of water flowing through the system. Sensors measure both the flow in the pipes and the amount of moisture in the soil, while valves are used to adjust the flow as required.

Delivering water

In the farmer's fields, irrigation water is supplied to the soil along the surface, underground, or through sprinklers. At the surface, the water may be applied to crops along furrows or by using controlled flooding.

Fields watered by flooding should be fairly flat. The fields are often divided into strips by raised banks. Flood irrigation is cheap and needs no special equipment. However, the raised banks need a lot of work to maintain. Flood irrigation

is used to water cereal crops such as wheat, rice, and barley, and also in orchards. Furrow irrigation is used for crops grown in rows, such as potatoes, corn, and cotton. This method is cheap and can be used on sloping land.

Underground irrigation delivers water directly to the subsoil where crops have their roots. The ground must be fairly level, and the topsoil must be porous (full of holes that allow air to penetrate). Water can also be supplied underground using pipes, but this method is expensive. Underground irrigation systems have to be checked frequently to make sure the soil does not become waterlogged.

Sprinkler systems are increasingly used in farming. They spray water from hoses or pipes suspended above the crop or are laid along the ground. Some systems are constructed in a fixed framework called a solid set. This covers the whole field. Solid sets are used for watering fruit trees and some other crops that need a lot of water, but they are difficult to move.

Most modern sprinklers are designed so they can be moved easily, or move automatically. The most common automatic mobile sprinkler is the center-pivot type. This consists of a long pipe fitted with sprinklers and fixed to a rotating

LOOK CLOSER

Traditional ways to raise water

In ancient times, farmers used different methods to raise river water to their fields. In Egypt, a device called the shaduf was common. It resembled a seesaw with a bucket at one end and a weight at the other. A machine called a bucket, or Persian, wheel was also widely used. This was a wheel fixed in an upright position with its base in the river. A line of pots or buckets was fixed around the wheel rim. As the wheel turned, the containers scooped up water and then tipped it into a trough at the top. The trough fed an irrigation channel. The wheel was often connected to a drum turned by an ox or donkey. In eastern Asia, bucket wheels were powered by small windmills. In the third century B.C.E., Greek scientist Archimedes (287–212 B.C.E.) invented a screw for raising water. It consisted of a cylinder with a large screw inside. One end of the cylinder was dipped in water. The farmer turned a handle attached to the screw to raise water up the tube. All three devices are still used in various places around the globe.

pivot. Such sprinklers can water a circular area up to 400 acres (160 hectares) in size. All sprinkler systems require a plentiful supply of relatively clean water so they do not clog up quickly. They are expensive to install and have to be maintained regularly, but they deliver irrigation water efficiently and can be used on steep slopes. They are also used to apply fertilizers and pesticides.

Drip irrigation is similar to the sprinkler method but delivers water to the crop even more efficiently. Water is applied through plastic pipes pierced with tiny holes at regular intervals. Each crop plant is carefully positioned near a hole, so water trickles out to the roots. Drip irrigation is expensive to install, but wastes very little water. This method is becoming widespread in dry countries such as Israel.

Drainage

Crops do not grow well in poorly drained soil, so drainage systems are often set up. The main purpose of drainage is to prevent the soil from becoming waterlogged and unsuitable for

In many parts of the world, rice is grown in irrigated fields called paddy fields. In Asia, these fields are terraced.

farming. In the United States, especially in the east, fields are most likely to get waterlogged in spring. Drainage also helps prevent farmland from becoming too salty, which is a problem in dry regions. Where large quantities of water are used to irrigate the soil, salt builds up over time because almost all irrigation water contains some salt. Drainage helps prevent the buildup of salt by flushing it through the soil.

There are two main types of drainage systems: surface and underground systems. In the surface systems, channels are dug to allow the water to drain into collecting ditches. Crops may be planted in shallow channels to save space.

In underground systems, water is usually carried away from the subsoil in pipes laid below the level reached by plant roots. Irrigation engineers study soil type and the depth of underground water sources to decide how deep to lay the drains. Alternatively, machines called mole plows are used to dig channels in the subsoil. Mole plowing is cheap but the drains have to be redug every few years as pipeless channels tend to collapse.

CHECK THESE OUT:
✔AGRICULTURE ✔CANAL ✔CROP FARMING
✔DAM ✔WATER RESOURCES

Laser

A source of intense, regular waves of light

Cutting machinery, CD players, surgical implements, and weapons systems all use laser technology. This technology is based on intense beams of laser light. Laser beams are very narrow—so narrow that they can be focused to a diameter of less than 0.001 inch (0.25 mm). These concentrated laser beams are also very powerful. They can weld metal, cut through diamonds and perform surgery. Laser light can do this because it has properties different from those of other types of light.

Concentrated light

Normal light does not travel in straight lines. It spreads out the farther it gets from its source. For example, the farther a planet in the solar system is from the Sun, the less sunlight hits it, because the light spreads out. Similarly, the farther an object in a room is from an electric lightbulb, the less light reaches it because light spreads as it travels from the lightbulb. However, laser light is different. It travels in parallel lines

Laser beams are now widely used in displays. Here, lasers pierce the sky as part of the Christmas decorations in San Francisco's Union Square.

and spreads out very little. Unlike sunlight or light from an electric lightbulb, laser light does not diminish as it travels from its source.

Waves of light

Laser light also differs from normal light in other ways. All light travels in waves. Just like the waves in the sea, light waves have peaks and troughs. The distance between one peak and the next is called a wavelength.

Light from a source such as a flashlight is a jumble of waves made up of all the colors of the rainbow. Each color has a different wavelength of light. However, laser light has one wavelength and color. Such light is called monochromatic (MAHN-uh-kroh-MAT-ik). Each wave of laser light is exactly in phase, which means that the peaks and troughs of one light wave are lined up exactly with the peaks and troughs of another light wave. The waves all reinforce each other. Such waves of regular light are called coherent.

Making laser light

Particles of light are called photons. These particles are released by atoms (the building blocks of all matter). The nucleus (center) of an atom is surrounded by smaller particles called electrons. The electrons orbit the nucleus. Electrons can jump from a high-energy orbit, far from the nucleus, to a low-energy orbit, near the nucleus. To make a working laser, there must be a large number of atoms with electrons in the same high-energy orbit. This collection of "excited" atoms is called the lasing medium. When an electron from one of these atoms jumps from the high-energy orbit to an orbit of lower energy, the atom releases a photon. The photon then collides with another atom in the same high-energy orbit. The electron jumps to the low-energy orbit, and the

Lasers can be used to cut into very tough materials—here, steel is being sliced into sections for shipbuilding.

atom releases an identical photon. The two identical photons then collide with more atoms, creating more identical photons. This process is called stimulated emission and gives the laser its name: light amplification by stimulated emission of radiation. The photons that are released by stimulated emission are exactly the same, but they are emitted in all directions. To be of use, they must be focused in one direction. To do this, there are two mirrors inside the laser, one at each end of the lasing medium. Photons bounce off the mirrors and travel back and forth through the lasing medium. The photons collide with more excited atoms. This process triggers the release of more identical photons.

One mirror at the end of the laser reflects perfectly. All the photons bounce off this mirror and trigger the release of more photons in the lasing medium. However, the mirror at the other end lets some photons through. These escape to form the beam of laser light.

Different lasers

One difference between lasers is the wavelength of the light produced. Other differences include the type of lasing medium used and the way that the atoms are excited. Solid-state lasers are well equipped to create short, intense pulses of laser light. Pulsed lasers produce large energy outputs in pulses that last for a fraction of a second. Different lasing mediums are chosen to produce the desired wavelength, the power output, and the pulse duration of the beam of laser light. Most gas lasers consist of visible red light. Some gas lasers, such as the carbon dioxide laser, do not produce visible light. Instead, they emit longer wavelength waves, such as microwave radiation. These are extremely powerful lasers.

Semiconductor, or diode lasers, are a common type of laser. They are very weak but small, highly efficient, and cheap. Excimer lasers use reactive gases such as chlorine and fluorine mixed with inert gases like xenon. These lasers produce ultraviolet light. Dye lasers use complex organic dyes as the lasing medium. They produce laser light with a wide range of wavelengths.

Cutting lasers

Lasers are used as heating and cutting tools in manufacturing and surgery. A laser beam can be so intense it can cut through metal. Carbon dioxide lasers emit infrared waves that cut through metal by melting it. Surgeons use lasers to cut into body tissues or kill cancerous cells by heating the water inside them. Other lasers join cells together deep within the body. The surgeon controls the power of the laser by altering the focus of the beam. This helps prevent damage to nontarget tissue. A tightly focused beam acts as a cutting tool, while an unfocused laser beam joins cells together over a wider area.

Compact discs

Compact discs, or CDs, use lasers to record and read digital information, such as music or a computer file, on the surface of a thin disc. Digital information is represented by a sequence

HISTORY

The development of lasers

1917 German-born U.S. scientist Albert Einstein explains how lasers could work.

1954 U.S. scientist Charles H. Townes and research scientists at Columbia University develop a maser, a laser that emits microwaves rather than visible light.

1958 U.S. physicist Gordon Gould invents the laser. He holds patents on laser uses.

1960 U.S. scientist Arthur Schawlow from Bell Telephone Laboratories, together with Townes and his team, develops a gas laser.

1960 U.S. scientist Theodore Maiman develops the first working model of a laser at the Hughes Research Laboratories in California.

1962 U.S. scientist Robert Hall develops the first semiconductor laser.

of numbers. The number code consists of just two numbers, 0 and 1, and is called binary code. To store information on the CD, a laser beam cuts into a thin metal layer under the plastic coating covering the disc. The metal becomes covered with microscopic indentations called pits and smooth areas called flats. To read the data, another laser beam passes over the surface of the CD. When the laser passes over a flat, it reflects

CORRECTING VISION WITH LASERS

1) A flap is cut on the surface of the eye, called the cornea. The flap is lifted back.

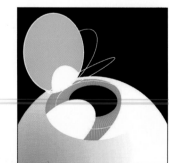

2) A laser is used to vaporize part of the middle cornea. This treatment alters the shape of the cornea.

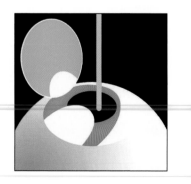

back onto a sensor. The sensor interprets the flat as the binary number 1. When the beam passes over a pit, the laser reflects away from the sensor. This represents the binary number 0. A CD player or computer then transforms the binary data into music or computer data.

Fibers and scientific instruments

Light can carry more information than radio waves because it has a higher frequency. Laser light is ideal for this purpose. Long thin tubes of glass or plastic, called optical fibers, can carry light long distances without interference. Even over huge distances, the intensity of the laser light means there is little reduction in signal quality. Lasers are also used in radio and satellite communications.

Laser light is useful as a measuring tool. Pulses of laser light can be aimed at a distant target where a mirror reflects it back to the sender. A high-precision clock then measures the interval between the pulse sent and returned. In this way, the distance between target and sender can be measured accurately. This technique was used to measure the distance to the Moon using mirrors left by astronauts on the U.S. Apollo missions.

Pulsed lasers let scientists look at processes that take place very quickly. The laser pulse acts like a camera flash, lighting up the scene for a tiny fraction of a second. In this time, the laser produces a hologram to represent the scene. Using these holograms, scientists are able to study rapid chemical reactions or the movement of fluids in detail.

INTO THE FUTURE

Lasers in the future

Scientists at the USAF Advanced Concepts Division are looking to use lasers as a means of propulsion. They aim to launch tiny laser-powered microsatellites into space. A laser would trigger an explosion to propel the microsatellite forward. Computer scientists are exploring the possibility of running computers using lasers. Instead of electrical signals, data would consist of different wavelengths of pulsed laser light. Such computers would be very fast.

Weapons

Lasers have transformed warfare. Lasers are used as extremely accurate targeting systems. Simple laser-guidance systems are mounted on rifles. The laser beam creates a bright spot on the target before the bullet is fired.

More advanced laser systems, such as those used to guide missiles, focus the laser beam onto the target. The missile is able to detect the reflected laser light and steers itself to impact. Lasers have also been developed as weapons. The United States Air Force (USAF) has developed a new laser weapons plan called the Attack Laser program. This will use huge lasers mounted on aircraft equipped with missile detection and targeting systems to destroy short-range missiles.

CHECK THESE OUT!

✔COMPACT DISC ✔FIBER OPTICS ✔HOLOGRAPHY

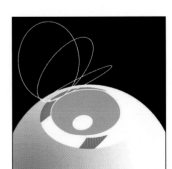

3) The flap cut from the cornea is folded back carefully across the eye.

4) The eye is left to heal. The altered shape of the cornea improves the person's vision.

Launch Site

A facility for launching rockets into space

Launch sites, or spaceports, are like airports for rockets. The launch vehicles (rockets) lift off from launchpads, supervised from a control center located a safe distance away. Elsewhere on the site, engineers fit the parts of the rockets together and prepare satellites and space probes for missions. Spaceports also contain facilities where astronauts prepare for their journeys.

Launch site locations

Space agencies choose their launch site locations carefully. Launching rockets can be dangerous, so launch sites cannot be built near cities. As they climb into the air, many launch vehicles drop the booster rockets that helped them to lift off. The area under the rocket's flight path must be free of people and buildings so the boosters can fall safely. Many launch sites are built on the coast so boosters can fall into the sea.

Most launch sites are also built at low latitudes (close to the equator). The Kennedy Space Center is based in Florida, while the European Space Agency's facility is at Kourou, French Guiana. Building a launch site near the equator is advantageous, because the planet's surface moves more rapidly there as the Earth rotates. This extra speed gives rockets a boost at lift-off. A vehicle launched into space must overcome the pull of gravity. The greater its speed, the higher the orbit it can reach. Earth's surface moves at about 1,000 miles per hour (1,600 km/h) at the equator, providing a useful kick start.

Assembly facilities

Most launch sites have assembly buildings where engineers build launch vehicles. Different parts of the vehicles are made in distant factories and shipped to the site. At the main Russian launch site, the Baikonur Cosmodrome in Kazakhstan, engineers assemble each rocket horizontally. Then, they mount the assembled rocket on railroad trucks, move it to the launchpad, and push it upright ready for launch.

At Cape Canaveral, in Florida, the assembly of most vehicles takes place in huge hangars close to the three main launch complexes. Engineers assemble the rockets vertically, then move them onto the launchpads. Titan rockets, the largest unpiloted U.S. rockets in use, are assembled in the nearby vertical integration building. This hangar can house four rockets at various stages of preparation. Assembled Titans travel to another building where booster rockets are fitted. Then, completed rockets move onto their launchpads.

The launchpad

The carefully timed series of events that lead up to a launch is called the countdown. Steel towers and girders hold the rocket safely upright on the pad during countdown and launch. These towers carry the walkways that enable engineers to prepare the rocket for launch. The towers also hold fuel pipelines, cameras, and other equipment. At some sites, the towers are fixed; at other sites, they are movable. The main launchpads at Baikonur have a series of movable towers. These rise up from the ground and lock into place around the vehicle.

Launch Complex 39 at Kennedy Space Center originally had no permanent tower. The Saturn V rockets that launched the U.S. Apollo Moon missions in the late 1960s and early 1970s arrived at the launchpad on a mobile launch platform. The crawler transporter that carried the platform lowered it onto a concrete base. Then, the crawler collected a mobile service structure, which supported the rocket during launch preparations.

HIGHLIGHTS

- Many launch sites are located near the equator where rockets gain extra speed from Earth's spin.

- Towers on the launchpad support the rocket before its launch.

- The series of events leading up to a rocket launch is called the countdown.

Countdown and launch

Preparations for most launches begin weeks or months ahead. At Kennedy Space Center, these preparations lead to the roll-out of the space shuttle. Carried on a giant crawler transporter, the shuttle travels from the vehicle assembly building to its launchpad at Launch Complex 39. The shuttle can stand on the launchpad for several weeks. Launch Complex 39 has two launchpads. These are upgraded versions of the pads once used for Saturn V launches. Each has a fixed service structure (FSS) with a tower

247 feet (75 m) high. This has swinging arms that lock into place to support the shuttle. It provides access to the orbiter, the airplanelike part of the shuttle that goes into space. It also carries fuel lines that deliver liquid hydrogen and liquid oxygen fuel to the shuttle's main tanks.

Each launchpad also has a rotating service structure (RSS). This swings into place behind the orbiter and allows access to the payload (cargo) bay and the orbiter's onboard systems. It carries a payload changeout room, which attaches to the payload bay doors. This allows equipment and other cargo to be placed onboard before roll-out.

The countdown for a shuttle launch begins with the call to stations by the launch director. This usually happens around 40 hours before launch. It ensures that all members of the launch team are in place in the launch control center's firing room and ready for countdown. The later stages of the countdown are referred to by the amount of time left before takeoff. For example, the stage nine minutes before takeoff is called T–9 minutes (takeoff minus nine minutes).

At T–1 day, the RSS swings away from the shuttle. Communication links open to connect the shuttle with mission control at Johnson Space Center, Houston. Mission control manages the shuttle flight after launch. At T–6 hours, the shuttle's large external fuel tank is filled, and communication links open to connect the ground stations that monitor the shuttle after launch. The crew travels to the launchpad at T–2 hours 30 minutes. They enter the shuttle. Other personnel leave the pad. Two hours ten minutes later, the crew sets the onboard computers for the launch. At T–9 minutes, the ground launch sequencer (GLS) computer takes control of most of the countdown functions. The

A pre-launch test of the Mercury - Atlas 0 (MA9) *rocket on launch pad 14 at Cape Canaveral, Florida.*

Kennedy Space Center

The Kennedy Space Center (KSC) is located next to Cape Canaveral on the east coast of Florida. As the only U.S. launch site for piloted spacecraft, it is the base for space shuttle operations. During the Apollo Moon mission program, KSC's 52-story Vehicle Assembly Building (VAB) allowed four Saturn V rockets to be assembled at one time. It is now equipped for assembling the various parts of the shuttle system—the orbiter vehicle, the external fuel tank, and the solid rocket boosters. The assembly of these components takes place on a mobile launch platform. Its support towers hold the shuttle upright. After assembly, the platform and shuttle together weigh more than 5,500 tons (5000 metric tons). A two-story vehicle called the crawler transporter carries them to the launchpad at a speed of 1 mile per hour (1.5 km/h).

shuttle's data recorders start up. The FSS's orbiter access arm swings clear of the shuttle at T–7 minutes 30 seconds. The solid rocket booster ignition system prepares for firing at T–5 minutes. In the final minute, the firing room instructs the shuttle's computers to begin the launch sequence at T–31 seconds. At T–16 seconds, the sound suppression system floods the pad with water to absorb engine noise vibrations. This

A perfect launch of the space shuttle **Discovery** *at Kennedy Space Center, in Florida.*

stops reflected engine noise from damaging the shuttle. At T–10 seconds, the command "main engine start" is given. Flares beneath the main engines burn off any hydrogen vapor collected there. This prevents uneven ignition of the fuel. Valves open to allow fuel into the engine pumps.

The main engines ignite at T–6.6 seconds and gradually increase to full power. At T–0 seconds the solid rocket boosters ignite. Explosive bolts that hold the shuttle above the launchpad explode to free it from its supporting arms. Gaining speed, the shuttle clears the top of the FSS at T+7 seconds and mission control at Houston takes over from the firing room.

CHECK THESE OUT!
✔ LAUNCH VEHICLE
✔ ROCKET
✔ SPACE STATION

Launch Vehicle

A rocket that carries a spacecraft into orbit

Launching a spacecraft into Earth orbit, or farther into space, requires a tremendous amount of power. Jet engines do not produce enough power to do this. They also cannot travel into space, where there is no air, because they need oxygen to burn their fuel. Rocket engines, which are powerful enough to carry spacecraft into orbit, carry their own supply of oxygen so they can operate in the airless vacuum of space.

Getting into orbit

To launch a satellite or probe into space, the launch vehicle has to overcome the pull of Earth's gravity. The pull of gravity reduces as an object gets farther away from Earth. If an object can travel fast enough, Earth's gravity will not be able to slow it enough to pull it back. This speed, called the escape velocity, is nearly 7 miles per second (11.2 km/s) on Earth.

Most launch vehicles place their payloads (satellites or space probes) into a low Earth orbit. This is less than a few hundred miles above the surface and well within the influence of Earth's gravity. At this height, an object traveling at the right speed—the orbital velocity—will be moving too fast to be pulled back to Earth by gravity. However, it will not be going fast enough to shoot into outer space. It will stay in orbit.

Many satellites orbit just beyond the outer layers of the atmosphere at an altitude (height) of 130 miles (200 km). The orbital velocity there is roughly 5 miles per second (8 km/s), much lower than the escape velocity. Nearly all launch vehicles are designed to put payloads into this

orbit. An additional rocket stage attached to the payload can then boost it to a higher orbit if required, or send it off into space.

Multistage rockets

Most launch vehicles consist of a series of rocket stages. Each stage has its own fuel tanks and engines. The bottom stage fires first, to get the vehicle off the ground. When its fuel runs out, it drops away from the vehicle, and the engines of the next stage start up.

The Chinese Long March 2 (Chang Zheng 2) launch vehicle, which has placed many telecommunications satellites into orbit.

SATURN V LAUNCH VEHICLE

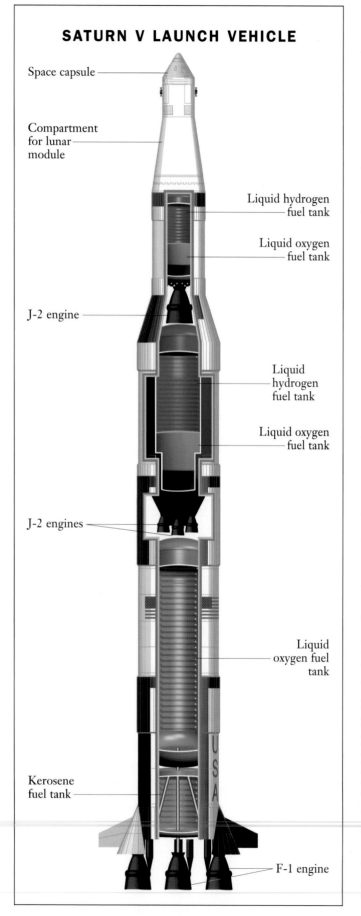

Space capsule

Compartment for lunar module

Liquid hydrogen fuel tank

Liquid oxygen fuel tank

J-2 engine

Liquid hydrogen fuel tank

Liquid oxygen fuel tank

J-2 engines

Liquid oxygen fuel tank

Kerosene fuel tank

F-1 engine

Without the weight of the empty first stage, the vehicle is much lighter. It needs less and less energy to keep on accelerating. Some rockets have three or four stages, each of which falls away when its task is complete.

Engines and fuels

Most large rocket engines generate thrust (the force that drives them) using two liquids. One liquid is a fuel, the other is called the oxidizer. The oxidizer is a source of oxygen, in which the fuel burns. Rocket engines use various liquid fuel-oxidizer combinations. The fuel and oxidizer burn in a combustion chamber at the top of the engine to create hot exhaust gases. These blast out through a nozzle at the base of the engine to produce the thrust that drives the rocket up.

Small rockets, and the booster rockets of large launch vehicles, are solid-fueled. They use a mixture of solid fuel and oxidizer held together by a binder such as synthetic rubber. This mixture is called a fuel grain. It is usually shaped into a cylinder that fills the casing of the rocket.

When ignited, the fuel grain burns down steadily like a giant firework. The force of the exhaust gas escaping through a nozzle at the base pushes the rocket forward. The booster rockets of the space shuttle are solid fuel rockets. Their fuel is powdered aluminum and their oxidizer is ammonium perchlorate.

U.S. launch vehicles

Most U.S. rockets used to launch spacecraft are expendable launch vehicles (ELVs). An ELV is used once. Its rocket stages fall into the sea or burn up in the atmosphere when their fuel has been used. ELVs might soon be replaced by the reusable launch vehicles (RLVs) now under development. Current U.S. ELVs include the Athena, Atlas, Delta, and Titan rockets. Titan IV, the largest Titan, is the most powerful unpiloted U.S. rocket. It is the latest in a long line of liquid-fueled Titan rockets that developed from an intercontinental missile design of the 1950s.

The largest rocket ever built was another U.S. vehicle, Saturn V. It was 363 feet (111 m) tall, and launched the Apollo missions to the Moon. The first stage was 34 feet (10 m) in diameter and 140 feet (42 m) high. It had five rocket engines in a cluster. Saturn V's second stage had five engines, and the third stage had a single engine. The Saturn V put the entire 52-ton (47 metric ton) Apollo payload on a path to the Moon. Later, the Saturn V launched *Skylab*, the first U.S. space station.

The space shuttle

The space shuttle is a unique launch vehicle because most of it is reusable. The only part that cannot be reused is the external fuel tank. The main part of the vehicle, the orbiter spacecraft, is mounted on this fuel tank. A solid rocket booster is attached to each side of the tank.

The external fuel tank feeds the orbiter's three main engines. These burn from lift-off until the shuttle reaches space, eight minutes later. Booster rockets burn for about two minutes after lift-off. Then, they separate from the external tank and parachute back down into the ocean. Ships

A Saturn 1B launch vehicle was used to carry Skylab 2 into orbit, on which experiments looking at the effects of space on humans were carried out.

LOOK CLOSER

Accidents and disasters

Most accidents happen before or during launch. The first fatal accident involving U.S. astronauts came in 1967. It happened during a routine test for the Apollo 7 mission at Kennedy Space Center. An electrical fault started a fire in the Apollo capsule, killing the three astronauts inside it. The most famous launch accident was the loss of the space shuttle *Challenger* in 1986. This accident killed seven astronauts. Soon after launch, a high-temperature jet of flame spurted from a fault in one of the booster rockets. It set off a series of failures that broke the shuttle assembly apart, and the orbiter crashed into the Atlantic Ocean.

---

recover them so that they can be refueled and used again. Shortly before the orbiter reaches orbital velocity, the external fuel tank drops away and burns up in the atmosphere. The orbiter's main engines shut down and it uses smaller engines for its final boost to orbit.

Other launch vehicles

The Proton is one of the most successful and powerful Russian rockets. Its first stage has six rocket engines arranged in a ring around a liquid fuel tank. One or two extra stages allow the vehicle to put payloads of up to 22 tons (22 metric tons) into low Earth orbit.

The European Space Agency uses Ariane rockets. The latest, Ariane 5, has a main engine and two solid rocket boosters. The engine and boosters produce enough power to take the vehicle to low Earth orbit. With a second stage added, Ariane 5 can boost a payload into a higher orbit.

The Chinese Long March rockets launch spacecraft for companies from many countries, including the United States. The Long March 3 can lift a 5.5-ton (5 metric ton) satellite into low Earth orbit.

CHECK THESE OUT!
✔LAUNCH SITE ✔ROCKET ✔SPACE PROBES

Leather

A tough, flexible material made from animal skins

Leather is used for many items, especially shoes and boots, despite the range of artificial materials available. It is normally made from cattle hides. Deer, goats, pig, and sheep skins are also turned into leather, and alligator, ostrich, shark, and snake skins are also occasionally used. Some leather, made from buffalo or cow hides, is very strong. Calf, buckskin, and kid skins from young goats make softer leather. Different treatments are used to produce patent leather, nubuck, and suede.

Making leather

The process of making leather from an animal skin has changed little over the centuries. After removal from the animal, the skin is cured by soaking in salt water. This toughens and cleans the skin. The skin is then washed in pure water to remove dirt and loosen the skin and hair.

Next, the leather is tanned. Chemicals called tannins, derived from trees such as chestnut, hemlock, mangrove, oak, and quebracho are mixed with water and applied to the skin. Chromium salts are sometimes used to make leather resistant to heat and water.

The tanned leather is then dyed. More than 100 color dyes are used on leather. Once colored, the leather is softened and made more flexible using soap or grease. The smooth surface is then polished and buffed. The amount of finishing depends on the thickness and quality of the leather, and whether it is glossy or dull.

Uses of leather

Leather is commonly used for bags, belts, gloves, jackets, pants, skirts, and briefcases. Reins and saddles for horse-riding are usually made from toughened leather. Baseballs and footballs often have leather covers. Industry also uses leather. The bearings of drive belts on trucks, buses, and automobiles are protected by leather seals. Furniture and automobile interiors often have luxury leather covers, while bookbinders have used leather to cover books for thousands of years.

Making leather is expensive, and leather items often cost more. Synthetic substitutes are cheaper to make and buy. Leatherette was an early substitute made from cloth coated with an elastic polymer like PVC or rubber. PVC looks and feels like leather.

CHECK THESE OUT!
✔ DYES AND DYEING
✔ FOOTWEAR
MANUFACTURE

Workers unload leathers from a tanning machine.

Glossary

•y A mixture of metals.

:sthetic (a-nuhz-THET-ik)
>rug that causes a loss of sensation
a a part of the body, or makes
patient unconscious through
1 operation.

ibody A protein made from white
lood cells that attacks foreign
odies in an immune response.

icoagulant A chemical that
ops the blood from clotting.

igen (ANT-i-juhn) A protein
carbohydrate on the surface of
foreign body that elicits an
imune response.

in A plant growth hormone.

A single unit of binary data; can
either 0 or 1.

e A group of eight binary digits
ocessed as a unit by a computer.

itation The formation of tiny
abbles of gas, for example around
e tops of hydrofoils.

onometer (kro-NAHM-uh-tuhr)
n accurate 18th century timepiece
at allowed sailors to work out
eir longitudinal position.

t Clumping of blood platelets.

g The resistance of air or water
the movement of objects.

ape velocity The speed that must
reached before a rocket can
cape the pull of a planet's gravity.

flail A free-swinging stick attached
to a wooden handle that farmers
once used to beat cereal crops;
this separated the grain from
the stalks.

germination When seeds, such
as cereal grains, begin to sprout
shoots and roots.

hormone Biological messenger
chemical.

hydraulic (hy-DRAW-lik) **system**
System driven by the
incompressability of fluids
such as oil or water.

hydroelectricity Electric power
produced by harnessing the
movement of water in rivers
and tides.

hypocaust A Roman underfloor
heating system with an underground
furnace; a series of tile flues
distributed the heat.

ignition (ig-NI-shuhn)
Causing something to catch alight,
such as diesel in an engine.

insulation Material that limits or
halts the passage of heat, sound,
or electrical current.

latitude Location north or south
of the equator.

lift Forward and upward force
produced by the shape of a wing that
keeps an airplane airborne.

longitude Location east or
west around the globe.

monochromatic (MAHN-uh-kroh-
MAT-ik) (*light*) Light of one
wavelength and one color.

noise Unwanted deviations in or
interference with an electrical signal.

novaculite (no-VAHK-yuh-lyt)
A very hard fine-grained rock
used to make whetstones, which
are used to sharpen metal blades.

pathogen (PATH-uh-juhn) An
organism that causes disease in
another organism.

phagocyte (FAG-uh-syt) Cells in
the blood that engulf and destroy
foreign bodies.

pneumatic (noo-MAT-ik) **system**
A system driven by compressed air.

relative humidity The amount
of moisture in the air.

scythe A tool used to mow cereals
and grasses consisting of a long
curving blade fastened to a long
wooden handle.

semiconductor Material which
conducts electrical current poorly
when pure but allows more current
through when impurities are added.

thrust Forward-acting force
provided by an airplane or
rocket's engines.

torque (TORK) A force that
produces a rotation.

toxicity A measure of how
poisonous a chemical is.

Index

AIDS 366
allergies *365*, 366
antibodies 364–365
autogiros 344
autoimmunity 365–366
automobiles *376*, *377*
  cooling 337
  hydraulic systems 357
  ignition systems 362–363

Bar codes *367*
Bessemer, Henry 379, 380
binary code 367, 390–391
blood cells 364
breeding, plant 349–350

Carnegie, Andrew 383
cavitation 361
CDs (compact discs) 390–391
central heating 339–341
chronometers 328
Cierva, Juan de la 343, 344
clocks, atomic 329
Cockerell, Christopher 354
combines (combine harvesters) 332–333
conduction (heat) 338, 339, 368
convection 338, 339
crops 351
  irrigation **384–387**

Daimler, Gottlieb *376*, *377*
dams 358–359
drainage, land 387
drills 331

E-mail 374
engines
  ignition systems **362–363**
  rocket 395, 396

Ferries 354, 361

fiber optics 326, 391
food processors *352*, 353
fruit 333, 348–349
furnaces 379
  blast 379, 381–382

Geothermal energy 341
Gibbon, John H. 336
glass and glassmaking **324–326**
gliders **327**
Global Positioning System (GPS) **328–329**
grafting, plants 351
grain, harvesting 333
Grand Coulee Dam 359

Hand tools **330–331**
harvesting machinery **332–333**
hazardous waste **334**
heart-lung machines **335–336**
heat exchangers **337**, 341
heating systems **338–341**
heat pumps 341
helicopters **342–344**
HIV 366
holography **345–347**, 391
hormones, plant 351
horticulture **348–351**
household appliances **352–353**
hovercraft **354–355**
Howe, Elias 353
hybridization 350
hydraulics **356–357**
hydroelectricity **358–359**
hydrofoils **360–361**

hydroponics 350
hypocausts *340*

Ignition systems **362–363**
immunology **364–366**
information theory **367**
insulation **368**
integrated circuits (silicon chips) **369–370**
intensive care units (ICUs) **371**
Internet **372–374**
inventions **375–377**
irons 352–353
iron and steel 330, **378–383**
irrigation **384–387**
ISDN 373

Jenner, Edward *366*

Kilby, Jack 370

Lasers *345*, *346–347*, **388–391**
launch sites **392–394**
launch vehicles **395–397**
leather **398**
light 346, 389
longitude 328

Micrometers *330*, 331
microprocessors 370
modems 373

Noyce, Robert 370

Photons 389
pneumatics 357

pollination 349–350
power stations 358, 359, *359*

Radiation (heat) 338, 339, 368
radiators 337
refrigeration 337, 341
reservoirs 358–359, 384
rockets
  launch sites **392–394**
  launch vehicles **395–39**

Satellites
  and GPS *328–329*
  launch vehicles *395–39*
scythes 330, 332, *333*
semiconductors 369–370
sewing machines 353
shadufs 384, *386*
sickles 332, *333*
Sikorsky, Igor 343, *344*
silage 333
solar panels *338*, 341
space shuttles *393–394*, 3
spark plugs *363*
springs, hot 341
steel *see* iron and steel
surgery 335–336
  laser *390–391*

Tools 375
  hand **330–331**
transplants, organ 366

Vaccination *364*, 365, *366*
ventilators *371*

Waste, hazardous **334**
wood and woodcarving 3
World Wide Web (WW 372, 374

Zeiss, Carl 326

Page numbers in **boldface type** refer to main articles and their illustrations. Page numbers in *italic type* refer to additional illustrations.